THE ESSENTIAL GUIDE TO A LIVING WILL

How to Protect Your Right to Refuse Medical Treatment

B. D. Colen

PRENTICE
HALL
PRESS

New York   London   Toronto   Sydney   Tokyo   Singapore

PRENTICE HALL PRESS
15 Columbus Circle
New York, NY 10023

Library of Congress Cataloging-in-Publication Data

Colen, B. D.
   The essential guide to a living will : how to protect your right
to refuse medical treatment / by B. D. Colen.
      p.   cm.
   Includes index.
   ISBN 0-13-284662-4
   1. Right to die—Law and legislation—United States—States.
2. Right to die—Law and legislation—United States—States—Forms.
I. Title.
KF3827.E87Z953   1991
344.73'04197—dc20
[347.3044197]   90-39596
                                                    CIP

Designed by Richard Oriolo

Manufactured in the United States of America

10 9 8 7 6 5 4 3 2

First Edition

ACKNOWLEDGMENTS

The preparation of this book would have been next to impossible without the help of two persons: A. J. Levinson, former executive director of Concern for Dying, and Alice V. Mehling, former executive director of the Society for the Right to Die. Both gave freely of their expertise and advice, for which I thank them.

Kenneth Paul, managing editor of the New York Observer and a good friend, provided his usual criticism and advice, and the book is better for both.

CONTENTS

CONTENTS

INTRODUCTION

---

*D*o you want your state legislature to determine how you spend your final days? Do you want someone who has never even heard of you to decide whether you should or shouldn't be maintained on a respirator in a vegetative state? Do you want a local judge determining whether or not tube feeding is appropriate medical treatment for *you*?

If you answered "no" to any of those questions, then you not only need a Living Will but you need a very personal, specific Living Will. For the U.S. Supreme Court's decision in *Cruzan v. Webster* says that states may pass laws requiring "clear and compelling" evidence, the highest standard of evidence used in civil cases, before allowing the withdrawal of life-sustaining medical treatment. In its historic "right-to-die" decision the court *did* hold that competent adults have a constitutionally protected right to refuse any and all medical treatment. And the court also included artificial nutrition and hydration—tube feeding and fluids—in the definition of medical treatment. At the same time, however, the court held that states may set the standard for determining, once you are no longer competent, whether you would or would not want to make use of your right to refuse treatment.

Thus far forty-one states and the District of Columbia have Living Will laws. Some also have legislation allowing you to name a "healthcare proxy," someone who will make healthcare decisions for you should you no longer be able to make them. The Supreme Court's *Cruzan* decision does *not* void those laws. It does not *require* any changes in them. Those that were liberal prior to the decision will remain liberal and those that limited rights, rather than protected them, will remain restrictive unless the laws are changed. For the *Cruzan* decision opens the door for the same kind of state-by-state battles over end-of-life issues that we have witnessed over abortion. So now, as never before, you *must* protect your rights in writing, in advance—unless you want to end your life as a prisoner of medical technology.

A few years ago, when Karen Ann Quinlan—the young New Jersey woman at the center of the nation's first "right-to-die" case—finally died after a decade in a persistent vegetative state (PVS), I asked George Annas, professor of Health Law at Boston University's Schools of Law and Public Health, what words or phrase he instantly associated with the name Karen Ann Quinlan. His reply? "Don't want to be like." And that, I would hazard a guess, is why you have purchased this little book. You may not know much about Living Wills, and you may not know much about the legality or ethical ramifications of withholding care from the hopelessly ill, but you probably know enough to say, as Annas did, "I don't want to be like Karen Ann Quinlan." Like most of us, you know that if you had a chance to choose the manner in which you will die, you would choose to die peacefully in your sleep. Denied that, you know that you want to "die with dignity," whatever that may mean to you individually. And thus we come to the purpose of this book, and a confession on the part of the author.

For a number of years I was opposed to the use of Living Wills. I wrote a number of articles and columns on the subject, warning readers that the documents were vague, dangerous, useless, and unnecessary. I worried that they were so vaguely worded that they could be used to terminate the life of an unconscious accident victim who would, with proper supportive intervention, recover to lead a relatively but not entirely normal life. I believed them to be useless because most state laws intended to legitimatize the Living Wills were little more than directives to physicians to "consider" a patient's wishes if a Living Will existed, and even then to consider the document only if it was worded in a certain way, drawn up within a certain period of time, and witnessed by a legally specified number of persons.

Even more important than any of those considerations was the fact that I naively believed that Living Wills were unnecessary. I had faith in the medical community's willingness and ability to, "above all, do no harm." I believed that doctors would have the knowledge and courage to stop a treatment when that treatment was no longer of any use to the patient—and I don't mean "of any use" in a vitalist sense, simply maintaining physical existence for its own sake, I mean "of any use" in the sense of helping the patient to recover to a state in which the patient would be willing to live.

I was not completely off base in this belief. There were even then, more than fifteen years ago, thousands of physicians who knew that the right to practice medicine carries with it the responsibility to know when to stop practicing on a given patient. There were then, and there are now, thousands of doctors who are willing to follow the wishes of patients when the patient, or those responsible for the patient, says it is time to step aside and allow the natural process of dying to conclude. Even the august American Medical Association (AMA), a body known for its extreme conservatism on most issues, issued in 1986 an official position paper condoning the withdrawal of all medical treatment and intervention, including what is euphemistically known as nutrition and hydration—food and water—in cases in which the patient is *either* dying *or* vegetative with no hope of recovery.

But the fact that the AMA took this stand and the fact that there are thousands of dedicated, courageous physicians does not mean that all, or even most, physicians and institutions will grant a patient's wishes when it comes to ending treatment. As I spent more and more time reporting on these issues and cases, I began to rethink my position on the Living Will and, today, I find myself writing this book. After all, although there may be thousands of physicians who understand that withdrawing care from the hopelessly ill is an integral part of the practice of medicine, there are countless thousands who still fail to grasp that simple fact. You may think that, because you have only read about a handful of "right-to-die" court cases, perhaps you have only heard of the *Cruzan* and *Quinlan* cases, that most of these fights have been settled at the bedside. Unfortunately, there have been more than 125 of them all around the country. And most involve the very issues resolved more than fifteen years ago in the *Quinlan* case.

So although I still do not believe that any Living Will is an ideal document and I still do not believe that having such a statement of purpose will guarantee you the treatment or lack of treatment that you wish, I *do*, however, believe that preparing a Living Will and a Durable Power of Attorney—which will be explained in detail later in this book—is the *only* way you have even a reasonable chance of being cared for in the manner you choose. Preparing a Living Will now will not guarantee that your family members or attorney will not have to go to court to enforce your wishes, but it will certainly make that eventuality far less likely. And, should a court fight become unavoidable, having a well-drawn Living Will will provide physicians, hospital administrators, or judges with little doubt what you would be requesting yourself were you competent to make a request for yourself.

One

THE NEED

*F*rom a medical standpoint, life and death used to be the simplest of concepts. Life began when you took your first breath and death occurred when you exhaled your last. There was no debate over the point at which life begins. What we could see, was. What we couldn't see, wasn't. And so it was with death. You were dead when someone said you were. That's right, when someone *said* you were. After all, as recently as the turn of the century, if the doctor couldn't detect a heartbeat, he declared the patient dead. Oh, high-tech medicine might have intruded in the form of the doctor holding a mirror beneath the patient's nostrils in the hope of detecting a faint breath. But in that simpler age, everyone knew that you were dead when you were dead. Because medical science was not yet able to artificially sustain the main organ systems, the concept of brain death did not exist.

There was, in fact, no need to differentiate between the death of the brain and the death of the heart. Death was death was death. And it didn't take a doctor to diagnose it, either. In 1900, virtually everyone except wards of the state died at home, in their own beds. While many deaths were attended by a Norman Rockwellesque family physician, most were not. So a family member or friend told the doctor that the patient had died, rather than the other way around.

Such apparent casualness with death was not confined to the days of our great-grandparents. As recently as 1949 less than half of America's annual deaths occurred in hospital beds. As we entered the 1950s and the beginning of the Age of Techno-Medicine, half of all Americans still were dying in their own beds, attended by family members. Hard as it is to believe now, just three short decades ago death was still considered a part of everyday life, albeit not necessarily a welcome one. Dying was considered part of living and took its natural place on an uninterrupted continuum that began with birth and ended with the moment of death. Because half of all deaths occurred outside the hospital, death was something familiar to most people: Rare was the individual who had not at least been present at the deathbed of a parent or grandparent. Those were the days in which pneumonia was still viewed as "the old man's friend," an infection that would hasten, rather than prolong, the process of dying once it had already begun. And then came technology.

Today, rather than dying at home, almost all of us are dying in hospitals and nursing homes, cared for at best, maintained at worst, by strangers. It would be bad enough were we to be escorted from this world by caretakers who we did not even know. But, even worse, those caretakers often view death and the dying process in a way vastly different from the way in which we view it. Although we may indeed consider death a friend, providing an escape from a painful, debilitating illness such as cancer, or as an ending and final escape from the cruel ravages of Alzheimer's disease, these caretakers view death as the ultimate enemy, to be fought with *your* dying breath. Each year, about 2 million of us die, and the professionals caring for us in our final months, weeks, days, and hours view those deaths as 2 million personal defeats. For death, rather than pain and suffering, is the ultimate enemy to many healthcare professionals and probably to most physicians. After all, if we give them the benefit of the doubt—and set aside whatever feelings we may have about how much physicians earn—we have to believe that most physicians become physicians because they want to *help* their fellowman, and they are trained to believe that they are helping when they cure, not simply when they comfort.

What does all this have to do with the crowding of technology into the hospital room? A great deal. The development of kidney dialysis, heart pacemakers, sophisticated monitoring equipment, and—even more important—the refinement of what doctors and nurses call a ventilator and you call a respirator provided physicians at the bedside with a whole new arsenal for their war against death. The refinement of the respirator and its movement from the operating room into the Intensive Care Unit (ICU) in the early 1960s raised the stakes in the war against death much as the explosion at Los Alamos raised the stakes in global warfare—the rules and risks would never be the same again. These new technologies gave the physician what he had never had before: devices with which he could actually postpone death, put it on hold. If the patient's kidneys failed, the physician could just hook up the dialysis machine and the patient would be spared death by uremic poisoning. If the heart became arrhythmic, just install a pacemaker. And if the patient had the temerity to stop breathing, just jam a tube into her trachea, attach the tube to the respirator, and turn on the machine. Bingo! the patient would be breathing again. Forget, if you will, that the patient's organs were failing because she was in the final stages of metastasized lung cancer. Ignore, if you can, the fact that the patient had slipped into a coma three days before her lungs and kidneys shut down. After all, what was being accomplished here was a technological and medical miracle. Death was being cheated. The doctor was "winning" the war.

The problem, of course, was that these wonderful new technologies were creating a new class of patient—and the need for new definitions of death. We were entering what might best be called the Age of the Living Dead. It was now possible to sustain the physical existence of patients who were mentally dead. These were patients who would have been declared dead had they been in this condition a few short years earlier. They were unable to breathe without the aid of a mechanical respirator—they were unable to breathe with it in many cases, because the respirator was breathing *for* rather than *with* the patient. And, far more important from a humanistic standpoint, they were unable to think.

I do not simply mean that these patients were—and are—unable to work out calculus problems or deal with philosophical issues; they were "dead" from the brain stem up, which means they were unable to perceive or conceive *anything*. They were unable to relate in the simplest way to themselves or anything in the world around them. They had lost any and all of the characteristics we associate with the term *person*, but they were alive.

While the public was unaware initially of these incredible changes in medical technology, physicians themselves were aware of, and troubled by, them. In fact, as early as 1957 a group of anesthesiologists, confronted with the dilemma of treating patients in the operating room who would obviously "die" if the respirator used during surgery was turned off at the end of an unsuccessful operation, turned for guidance to Pope Pius XII. Is there, they asked the pontiff, a moral obligation to sustain life in hopeless cases? Is there a moral obligation to use "extraordinary means" to maintain the life of a patient who cannot in any way benefit from that life?

What even most Catholic clergy did not know at the time was that the church has a very "liberal" and time-honored position on the use of "ordinary" and "extraordinary" means to preserve life, one dating back to the Middle Ages. But wait, you say, if this technology first appeared on the scene about thirty years ago, how can the Catholic church have a position on its use dating back at least 600 years? As the pope explained to the bewildered physicians, the church was not considering uses of technology but morality, what is ultimately right and ultimately wrong. And in less "civilized" times, when men still burned each other—and women—at the stake, the person being burned was given one bucket of water, which they could request while being burned. The dilemma then facing the Church's moral theologians was whether the person being burned was morally obligated to request the water. Was the use of the bucket of water "ordinary," and was there, therefore, a moral obligation to call for the water and thus preserve one's life for a few moments more? No, came the humane reply, calling for a single bucket of water while burning at the stake would be "extraordinary," and thus was not morally obligatory, because the use of the water would not extend life, it would only extend the process—and the agony—of dying.

The pope explained to his audience of physicians that the Catholic church did not, and does not, require the use of extraordinary means to sustain life. Even if the case is not hopeless, but the means are so extraordinary as to impose an enormous burden, be it one of pain or even of overwhelming financial obligation, its use is not obligatory. If, for instance, a family member has cancer, and that cancer could be successfully treated, but only if the family sells its home to pay for that treatment, the sick family member would not be morally obligated to request, or accept, the treatment. By the same token, the pope explained, physicians were not morally obligated to use the new life-extending technologies in a purely vitalist fashion. That is, if the technology could be used in such a way that it would truly benefit the patient, as a patient with pneumonia might benefit from the use of a respirator for a few days, then the use of that technology was morally obligatory. If, however, the patient would not benefit from the use of the technology, as a chronically comatose patient would not benefit from the use of the respirator, then its use in such a case would be considered extraordinary and, therefore, would not be required morally.

All of this made perfect sense in 1957 and continues to make perfect sense today. One does not have to be a Roman Catholic to see the wisdom in the pope's statement. It simply does not make sense to waste resources or to make a patient suffer when there is no hope for reasonable recovery or extension of useful life. Unfortunately, many physicians—and most hospital administrators and attorneys—fail to see things that way. In the first place, as was already mentioned, physicians are trained to save "lives," not comfort the dying. And all hospital administrators and attorneys seem to think about these days is how to avoid legal difficulties that they, and only they, can only imagine.

Many hospital-based physicians, when asked to turn off a respirator in a hopeless case, will tell the patient's family members, "I'd really love to help you. But under the laws of this state, I simply can't. I could be charged with murder if I did." Well, the difference between "could be" and "would be" is astounding indeed. In the first place, there are only two groups of laws that deal with the question of turning off life-sustaining machinery, and those, in the states that have them, are so-called brain death statutes and laws regarding Living Wills. The first apply only to the procedures for declaring a patient brain dead—they have nothing to do with the appropriate use of medical treatments in a given case; the second outline for a physician what he must and must not do when a patient has a *valid* Living Will. Neither group of laws threatens physicians with homicide prosecution should they decide—using the same medical judgment that would lead them to believe a patient was not benefiting from a particular antibiotic—that a respirator was no longer of benefit to a patient.

Obviously a physician, like any other member of society, can be charged with murder if he or she violates the homicide laws. But this is where we come to the difference between "could be" and "would be." Not only has there *never* been a case of a physician being convicted of a crime in connection with the medically legitimate withdrawal of life-sustaining treatment, but there has, in fact, never even been a case of a physician being convicted in connection with a blatant mercy killing. In the entire history of this country, there has been only one incident in which an overzealous prosecutor charged two physicians with murder and conspiracy to commit murder after they acceded to the written request of a vegetative patient's family members and withdrew life supports. All charges were dismissed, however, before the case even came to trial. So although physicians practicing medicine in this litigious age may honestly fear they will be charged with murder for practicing medicine, the chances such a thing will actually happen are so slim as to be nonexistent.

Unfortunately, however, the fact that physicians are *not* charged with murder when they honor family or patient requests does not really help you much, because you still have to deal with the reality of a physician's fears and the ethical/legal climate in any given hospital. You are also forced to deal with the reality that, despite the widespread use of such rhetoric, there is no "right to die," constitutional or otherwise. Any person who aids another's suicide attempt may face prosecution. Which brings us to the concept and purpose of the Living Will.

You should think of a Living Will as a document in which you carefully explain your beliefs and desires concerning the use of medical interventions to extend the dying process and to sustain life in circumstances in which you would rather not live. The Living Will you prepare is your attempt to guarantee that the absolute right you have as a competent individual to refuse or agree to medical treatment be preserved should you no longer be competent. For while you are competent, you do not have a legal right to die, but you *do* have a right to refuse medical treatment. Unless a physician or hospital can either show that you are incompetent or the state can prove to a court that it has an overwhelming need to preserve your life—for instance, if you are the single mother of young children who would become wards of the state should you die—you can refuse treatment even if that refusal will lead to your death. Your Living Will would be designed to protect that right.

For a Living Will to be effective, it must be written or, even better, videotaped in such a way that no physician or hospital administrator will be able to stand before a judge and say, with a straight face, that it is not possible to determine what you would want given the circumstances at hand. The will has to be prepared in such a way that your intent is absolutely clear. And almost as important as the clarity of your intent is the need for the will to exhibit your understanding of the treatments and technologies you would or would not want used to sustain your life, and under what circumstances you would object, or agree, to their use.

Two

THE DOCTOR

*F*or you to understand better the absolute necessity of not only having a Living Will but of having one that is as *explicit* as it can possibly be, listen for a few moments to the director of an Intensive Care Unit (ICU) at a major university teaching hospital. While you may have an excellent relationship of many years' standing with your family physician, the ICU director is the individual who will be overseeing your care should you suffer a stroke, a heart attack, or become so ill that you need the kind of modern supportive care that can be provided only in an ICU. This particular intensivist (as they are called), whom we will call Nicholas Benjamin, is a kind, enlightened, relatively young individual. He is personally introspective and thoughtful, and he has given a great deal of time to considering the uses and misuses of medical technology to sustain the life of the hopelessly ill. In fact, *he* has a Living Will. He has given *his* family explicit instruc-

9

tions concerning the kind of care he would or would not want to receive should he be totally incapacitated. And yet, when asked whether he would honor a patient's Living Will, this is what he said:

"I don't think anything has changed in this state," which does not have a law regarding Living Wills. "There is a lot of case law here but I don't think a Living Will is something a doctor can be held accountable to. I don't think that I, or many other physicians, would feel comfortable in taking someone's documentary videotape of their statements at some other place, at some other time, without full recognition of what these things entail and what the prognosis might be. I don't know how valid that would be. For me, it would be an indication, as I would want for myself, of what my intentions are and were, and so from that point of view I think it carries a lot of weight. It helps me in terms of trying to understand that person and how far they would want to go under circumstances that I now know that they didn't know at the time they prepared the Living Will. In essence, what I'm saying is that I have a problem with the legality of it and with the repercussions if I do not do everything that is in the patient's best interest."

Dr. Benjamin, who is called upon every day to make decisions regarding the lives and deaths of dozens of patients in his unit, explained that he sees a basic conflict between what he views as his "role as a physician, the legal role, my perception of beneficence—which is to do what's in the patient's best interest—versus the patient's self-determination and autonomy, which is in essence what you have when you have a Living Will that says, 'This is what I want you to do.' So you try and give credence to the person's right to self-determination and their own personal rights in terms of expressing themselves as to their healthcare. But for me personally it would still create a major dilemma, because I don't think it would get me off the hook legally. I would still be compelled to use my best judgment at that particular point in time, given the circumstances under which the patient came in, to do whatever I would have to do. And that would entail for me, as it has in the past, trying to make the determination as to what the nature of the disease is, how much do we know about the extent of the disease, how much of it is reversible, and how far are we going to go to give that person a good shot to show us whether they can come back and have some kind of meaningful existence."

As he sat in a conference room off the ICU, he did not, of course, discuss what would happen should the patient survive without a "meaningful existence." That is somebody else's problem. Yours, for instance.

Instead, the physician said that "my policy, my feeling, my own personal ethics if you will, still dictate to me that I still have to have a feel for that individual, I still have to see what the response to therapy is, or was, or will be, before I pull back. If someone has end-stage cancer, and they're [falling apart] from chemotherapy on the floor, I would have difficulty going ahead. But many of my colleagues, the oncologists particularly, disagree with me."

But suppose, Dr. Benjamin was asked, you have a seventy-five-year-old woman brought in from a nursing home, who has suffered a severe stroke. Her daughter accompanies her in the ambulance and immediately tells you that she has had numerous conversations with her mother and her mother always said, quite explicitly, that she would not want to live if she could not care for herself. The daughter then hands you a videotape, made by her mother two years earlier, in which her mother says exactly what the daughter has reported and goes on to say, "I do not ever want to live if I become a burden to others."

The ICU director thought for a moment and then replied that "the bottom line is that if the family doesn't want us to do certain things, some things are easier not to do than others. If the patient comes in with a daughter, you don't know whether the daughter has the patient's best interest at heart, whether she's looking to inherit a million dollars, or what the hell's going on. You have to be very careful about family members making determinations about living and dying for patients, and you need time—I don't know this patient from a hole in the wall. Just because the daughter says she's a vegetable or a near vegetable and she has a tape. . . . I see the tape as being indicative of what the lady wanted, but when she enters the hospital she is not able to understand what could be done for her or not be done for her to give her a meaningful existence, or a quality of life that she tried to define earlier. So there's a lot to be left to the doctor's imagination. There are areas of gray. When you say she would not want to live if she couldn't take care of herself, what does that mean? Does it mean she'd want to do everything she could do at age twenty? Does it mean she'd be satisfied in a nursing home where she could wash herself and brush her teeth and go to the bathroom? Does it mean she's on a ventilator [respirator] and couldn't do anything? The big problem with Living Wills, among others, and don't get me wrong, I'm in favor of Living Wills, but the big problem is that they're vague. They're either too vague or they're too inflexible—that's the problem in a nutshell.

"The other issue," he said, "is the family. Families can give you some idea of what you might do, but I hesitate to use the family or a daughter or a cousin as the sole means by which I would determine how to proceed. Now a spouse I would give more credence to, but a spouse can be acting on misinformation or making the decision based on wrong information. And that's another responsibility that a physician has to decide on before she can make any hasty judgments about letting somebody die or not instituting a particular therapy—because once that decision's made, it has far-reaching and wide and severe repercussions. That's why our policy here has always been to give the patient the benefit of the doubt [medically], to act in the patient's best interest as *we* define it [emphasis added]. And, if at all possible, we consider other corroborative evidence from the patient's family physician, personal physician, or if there's a history of the patient being in the hospital here so we know something about them. Then we *can* make decisions about what should we do and what should we not do—and make sure that everybody's in agreement, because the minute you've got somebody who's not in agreement, then you've got problems. That was pointed up by the situation in California a couple of years ago when two guys got sued for murder. . . . So if there's any doubt, we do everything we can do."

The problem with the policy in Dr. Benjamin's ICU, and in many others, is that the policies contain a catch-22: Every patient who is admitted to the unit with any difficulty breathing is given respiratory support; if that means putting the patient on a respirator, then that is done automatically. The physician and his staff will not allow a patient to die as a result of respiratory failure, which he describes as an "awful death." However, once the patient is on the respirator, the machine will *never* be disconnected unless the patient no longer needs it or is declared dead. So if you need a respirator to breathe and end up in an ICU like this, your Living Will will be ignored automatically—at least initially.

And then we come to medical/ethical game playing. Respiratory death is an awful thing, so the best thing to do is get the patient on the respirator . . . which is when the game playing begins. For although Dr. Nicholas Benjamin will not turn off a patient's respirator, he says: "If the patient is in a vegetative state, or did not want certain things done, did not want to live in a state where there is *any* impairment, then we have choices about antibiotics, about blood, about blood products, about tube feedings, which is a whole other argument, but the main arguments revolve around pumping on the chest after the patient is intubated, agents used to maintain blood pressure, antibiotics, blood drawing, treatment and correction of electrolyte imbalances: All of these things need to be discussed item by item and case by case. We can do everything else short of turning off the respirator. We can decide not to draw blood, and then we won't know about electrolyte problems. We can do something about the feeding, because for me I can live with just giving minimal carbohydrates, we can decide not to give antibiotics, we can decide not to give blood and, therefore, not spot and treat electrolyte problems. I personally have no problem with not instituting another course of antibiotics when the patient becomes febrile. Once having had your best shot at it, I can say, medical opinion can say therapy and additional therapy would be futile and we have no obligation to give futile therapy. The respirator is futile therapy, in some manner of thinking, but if you stop the respirator the patient will die as a proximate result of your turning off the respirator. If I'm taking away a therapy that results in immediate death, I can't deal with that. But to decide out-of-hand that you're not going to do something initially, based on what a family member tells you . . . "

He shook his head. "Even with a Living Will, with the legal situation what it is, I think a doctor and a hospital would be on very shaky legal ground" if they failed initially to do everything they felt was medically dictated.

But then, he said, comes the question of Do Not Resuscitate (DNR), or so-called No Code orders, which he sees as being a different question from Living Wills. (*You*, however, *must not* make this distinction and *must* be explicit about Do Not Resuscitate orders when you prepare your Living Will.)

"The question of Living Wills is a separate issue," the physician believes, because "they can specify resuscitate, do not resuscitate, but you can only make that determination beforehand with great difficulty. You can make that determination after the fact, once the patient is on a ventilator, and that happens quite a lot, the decision to make a person DNR, after many things have been done, after an initial flurry to try and see what we can recoup. It comes to that very quickly in many cases. And that basically just revolves around pumping on the chest or not pumping on the chest, and you can get into No Codes, Slow Codes, Chemical Codes. It's an unofficial policy that's evolving, and it's usually one that's developed based on consensus, and the personal physician, the house staff, and the family have to agree before we can even talk about that kind of thing. But again, that's usually something that develops after the initial flurry, sometimes, in many cases, after the patient is intubated and has had a course of antibiotics, has had a course of therapy for the condition, so usually we're talking about several days to ten days to two weeks, or longer in some cases. Then we can make a determination that specific treatments are futile and that the patient has an irreversible process—and those are two key phrases: *futile treatment* and *an irreversible process*. And it's always done in conjunction with a consensus, especially the family. If anyone disagrees, then everything is done. And the same thing applies in reverse: Even though the daughter may say her mother wouldn't want something, if I, as a physician, don't feel I know the patient well enough and don't know the nature and extent of her disease well enough, I can't be bound by what the daughter says. I have to act in the patient's best interest, because I am the patient's ultimate advocate. That's traditionally what the patient-doctor relationship is. And no one should come between the doctor and the patient in that regard. And I, therefore, have to make that determination. No one can make it for me. No law can make it for me, unless there's a law that says Living Wills must be followed to the nth degree—then so be it."

Suppose the patient is being fed by a nasogastric tube—a tube that is snaked through the nose, down the esophagus, into the stomach—and the time comes when it is medically necessary to perform a gastrostomy, a surgical implantation of a feeding tube into the stomach. Will the physician force that on a family and patient? "I don't know that I would force a family that was against this to go through a surgical procedure. . . . I can live with that. Okay, let's play it the other way and give them what nutrition we can, even though it's inadequate. When I said I'd do everything, I don't mean to say that in all categories and all situations I'm going to forcibly carry medical treatment to the nth degree, I don't mean to imply that at all. I mean that when I have to make a judgment about life-saving measures and I'm getting mixed information from you, or a Living Will, or a daughter, I'm going to do what I have to do."

But again, he stressed, turning off the respirator is another matter. "In my view there is no way that I personally, ethically, medically, as an agent of the hospital, can be party to that without a legal decision. No matter what my personal feeling, my personal beliefs, my personal bias, and my own strong feeling about a Living Will, they have nothing to do with it. It has to do with my own sense of priorities and my own sense of legal responsibility and legal culpability, and the impact it could have on me personally, the hospital, and my family. It could come to that. The system is so bizarre that a personal decision made by me may be attributed to me and I may be held personally liable and my family, therefore, would not only be affected indirectly but directly, because my assets could become an issue. . . . I see the worst-possible-case scenario in everything that I do, even though personally, for myself, I agree with what you're trying to do and what you're saying. I don't want my family being bled to death financially, I don't want them agonizing for weeks or months over me as a vegetable—and you can document this because you have it on tape! It's a duplicity of thought, but it's a fact."

Although Dr. Benjamin's position may seem paternalistic and inflexible—there certainly are some physicians running

ICUs whose policies are much more liberal—he stressed one final point that is hard to disagree with no matter where you stand on the question of Living Wills, and it is one you should keep in mind: "The hospital is not the place to come if you want to be left alone to die."

Three

THE TECHNOLOGY

Rather than be discouraged by what you have read in chapter 2, you should consider it very carefully—on two distinct levels. On the first, you should remember what Dr. Benjamin said is true: You cannot plan, in advance, for every possible medical disaster that might befall you. You cannot truly know precisely what you would want done under every possible circumstance. *However*, you can carefully consider what outside limits you want to put on the medical care you may be given. You can give physicians, hospital administrators, attorneys, and judges a clear idea of what life means to you, of what being alive means, and a clear idea of the circumstances under which you *know*, as no one else possibly can, you would find death preferable to life. You can and must make it clear in your Living Will, written or video-taped, that you understand the kinds of technologies that might be used to save you, that you understand that you *might* have a shot at recovery were some of these technologies used, but that you are not willing to take the greater chance that you will not recover to lead a meaningful life.

If you are admitted to a hospital's Intensive Care Unit, you will be entering an environment in which everything is geared to preserving life at all costs. As Dr. Benjamin put it, "the basic premise behind the Intensive Care Unit is that there's something that's acutely wrong that's potentially reversible and, therefore, these patients could benefit from the special modalities, in terms of monitoring—especially intensive nursing and physician care—and that this hopefully will bear fruit in terms of the patient's overall outcome. Right off the bat you're talking about monitoring; you're talking about monitoring the heartbeat; the vital signs, such as pulse, temperature, and blood pressure; neurological status, as that may be applicable; and drawing blood and doing blood [tests] and doing cardiograms, as that may be appropriate. . . ."

In this ICU, and in many others, every patient has an intravenous (IV) line of some sort hooked up on admission. That way, even if the line is not needed initially, it is in place when it is needed and you can be given drugs or fluids faster than you could be if it were not ready. There are those who argue that such preplacing of IV lines is done for the convenience of the medical staff, rather than for your benefit. But if you think about it for a moment you'll realize that it may help you to have the line placed initially: It doesn't matter to the staff when they actually do the work.

You may have what is called an *arterial line* placed in the wrist to make it easier for the staff to draw blood samples on a frequent basis. Although placing the line is painful initially, once it is in place blood can be withdrawn subsequently with little discomfort to you.

You may be given what is called a *central venous access*, which means that you have a catheter—a tube—inserted in a large vein, usually the subclavian vein, or the internal jugular vein, or more likely, if you are less severely ill, you may have a *peripheral vein catheter* placed in the arm or the hand and have maintenance intravenous fluids started. That way, if you need medications in an emergency, the staff already has direct access to the circulation. Thus, in many ICUs the policy is that everybody gets an intravenous line, and the question of where that intravenous line goes is determined by the nature of the patient's illness.

In addition to having lines placed in veins or arteries to give you fluids and medications and draw blood, if you are admitted to an ICU you may well have a tube inserted in your urethral opening so that the staff can measure your urine flow. If you are lucky, you will be asked simply to urinate into a container and the contents will be measured. But if you are sick enough to be concerned about the terms of your Living Will, the odds are you will be subjected to a *Foley catheter*, which is inserted—"snaked," in hospital parlance— through the urethra directly into the bladder. The Foley allows for the minute-by-minute monitoring of urine flow— which is necessary to monitor kidney function—and, the ICU director says in a wonderful example of understatement, "it is uncomfortable."

An arterial line is a catheter or other line placed in an artery, usually in the wrist, farther up the arm, or in the groin. A so-called central venous line is usually placed in the neck. This access is often used to allow the insertion of a *Swan-Ganz catheter*, which is inserted—the staff will talk of "threading"—through a large vein in the neck and pushed through the vein into the right side of the heart where it measures pressures in the heart as well as in the pulmonary artery. To insert this catheter, the intensivist explains, a physician will "anesthetize the area, place a catheter, find the vessel, put a guide wire in through the skin, then make a small incision in the skin, basically a puncture, to allow the bigger wire to go in through the skin."

In this age of medical high-tech, it is unlikely that any hospital-based physician will agree to treat you if you refuse to submit to the various indignities and "discomfort"—the medical establishment's euphemism for pain—connected with monitoring. But if you feel strongly enough about this issue—to the point where you want to put your family members through the virtual necessity of going to court to see that your wishes are carried out—you should use your written and/or videotaped Living Will to spell out your objections to the use of *invasive monitoring* techniques.

If you are like most of us, you are not so much concerned about the basic indignities and discomforts that are a part of hospitalization. Rather, you are frightened that you may be "saved," kept alive physically long after your "spirit" is gone, through the use of a *respirator*—which physicians refer to as a *ventilator*—and tube feeding.

Not every patient in an ICU, or even every patient in a persistent vegetative state for that matter, needs to be attached to a respirator to breathe. Because breathing is regulated by the most basic portions of the lower brain, it is entirely possible that you could suffer a stroke or other "cerebral accident" that might entirely wipe out your higher brain functions, leaving you a vegetable by even physicians' definition, and yet you could continue to breathe.

Many ICU patients, however, either start out or end up needing supplemental oxygen, which may be delivered to the lungs in one of several ways, the simplest of which is the *nasal cannula*. The nasal cannula is, basically, a length of plastic tubing with two short prongs that are inserted in the nostrils. An elastic band that goes around the head holds the tube and prongs in place, and supplemental oxygen is delivered through the tube. This method is used for a patient who is capable of breathing on his or her own, but who needs more oxygen than his or her system is able to extract from room air.

An *oxygen mask*, which is not much different from the device you see demonstrated on airplane flights, straps over the nose and mouth and allows for the more carefully controlled delivery of higher volumes and concentrations of oxygen than is practical using the nasal cannula. However, this device, like the nasal cannula, is for patients whose lungs still function independently.

Patients who need even more oxygen than can be delivered adequately by mask or who are suffering from *respiratory failure*—their lungs are not functioning sufficiently well to oxygenate the blood and remove carbon dioxide from the system—are intubated and placed "on" the respirator, or ventilator. Even the ICU director you met earlier is willing to acknowledge that "intubation is major discomfort," but "in the extreme situation, where patients have extreme problems with inadequate oxygen in the blood, or where they have respiratory failure, they would be intubated and put on a ventilator, and one of the functions of a ventilator is to supply supplemental oxygen, up to 100 percent."

Intubation, the insertion of a tube into the trachea to allow the delivery of oxygen directly to the lungs, can be accomplished in one of two ways: through the nose or through the mouth and throat—and neither is pleasant. The so-called blind approach involves the insertion—shoving—of a thin tube up the nose, through the posterior pharynx, past the larynx (vocal cords) into the lower trachea. The physician attempting this procedure guides himself by listening to the patient's breath sounds. This is called the blind approach because the insertion of the tube is accomplished without the physician's looking down the patient's throat, and it requires insertion through the nose. As the ICU physician admits, "putting a tube in through the nose, which was not designed to have a tube put through it, can be more painful [than using a laryngoscope]. On the other hand, subsequently it seems to be better tolerated by the patient because there is less movement of the tube once it is inserted."

The more traditional method for intubating a patient is to use a *laryngoscope*—an instrument not unlike a vaginal speculum with a light and magnifying lens attached—to pass the tube down the throat. The trick for the physician is to get the tube into the trachea, rather than the esophagus, past the vocal cords, and then get it into a secure position where an inflatable cuff around the tube can be used to close off the airway. The inflatable cuff accomplishes two things: It prevents the patient from regurgitating material from the esophagus into the lungs, and it allows the positive pressure of the respirator to work. Neither the nasal tube nor the tube passed directly down the throat allows the patient to speak, because the tube interferes with the motion of the vocal cords and speech involves the passage of air past the vocal cords. Once the tube is inserted, there is no air moving back and forth past the vocal cords, and thus there is no sound. When the tube is removed, however, and the vocal cords are given a chance to recover from the battering they have undergone, the vast majority of patients regain their speech.

Understandably, the process of being intubated causes most patients to gag, because the back of the throat is touched and the gag reflex takes over. In some patients the feeling of gagging may pass very quickly. In others it may last for days or for as long as the tube is in place. "It's not a whole lot of fun being on a ventilator," ICU director Benjamin says, in his understated way.

One thing that can make being on a respirator an easier ordeal, particularly for a conscious patient, is to be anesthetized and undergo a simple surgical procedure called a *tracheostomy*. This involves making a cut through the neck and trachea, and implanting a very short piece of tubing and fitting that keeps the incision open once it heals. The tube from the respirator is then attached to the tracheostomy tube and the patient no longer has the discomfort of having a tube jammed down the nose or throat. This has the additional advantage of allowing a respirator-dependent patient to take food by mouth and to talk—and those are two enormous advantages.

The ventilator, or respirator—to which the other end of the tube is attached—is, basically, a pump or bellows that delivers a timed, volume- and pressure-controlled flow of carefully balanced gases to the patient's lungs. The machine takes over the work of breathing for the patient by forcing oxygenated air into the lungs and then allowing it to flow back out, removing carbon dioxide. The respirator forces the lungs to operate in an opposite manner from the way they operate naturally. When you take a breath on your own, your rib cage expands, your diaphragm goes down, and air is sucked into the lungs. The respirator, on the other hand, pumps air into the lungs, physically battering the cells at the same time it is providing oxygen to them. If a patient is on a respirator for a long period of time, usually for more than a few weeks, this battering may cause permanent damage to the lungs. And the high concentrations of oxygen used for respirator patients—up to 100 percent pure oxygen—cause *oxygen toxicity*. Cellular evidence of this oxygen toxicity can usually be detected within about twenty-four hours of a patient being put on 100 percent oxygen. Oxygen toxicity is what is known as a time-duration phenomenon: All people will eventually develop oxygen toxicity if they are exposed to high enough concentrations of oxygen for a long enough period of time.

There are several important things to remember about the respirator when you are preparing your Living Will and/or the videotaped document. In the first place, if you really think about it, you will probably come to the conclusion that there are circumstances in which you *would* want to be placed on a respirator, hellish as the experience might be: If it is used as a short-term support in a medical crisis, the respirator is indeed a miracle of modern medicine. For instance, if you develop pneumonia and are hospitalized, the use of the respirator would mean the difference between death by drowning—that is what a pneumonia death is—and a full recovery to whatever quality of life you had prior to becoming ill. You might have emphysema and reach the point where you needed a respirator permanently, but you were still in full control of all your senses and were able to get around with a portable respirator. This might be an acceptable quality of life for you, while it might not be for someone else. The same thing might be true if you had a neurological condition such as amyotrophic lateral sclerosis (ALS), also called Lou Gehrig's disease. Some individuals, such as the late Senator Jacob Javits, want to keep going. For them the respirator is a much-desired lifeline. You might feel this way. On the other hand, you may have the same disease but feel that you no longer want to live at the point when the use of a respirator becomes necessary. It is very important that you make distinctions such as these in your Living Will, in order both that your wishes will be clearly understood by your representatives *and* that no physician will be able to say that you simply made vague emotional statements and decisions prior to becoming ill, without understanding their ramifications.

Another issue that must be spelled out very carefully, and that you must fully understand, is the use of *artificial nutrition and hydration*—tube "feeding." If you are on a respirator, you *are* going to be fed by tube because you will not be able to take anything by mouth. This may be another of those line-drawing issues for you. You may feel that you would be willing to be tube fed for a short, set period of time, but that you would be unwilling to be sustained by this technology for any prolonged period of time. If that is the case, *define* prolonged. And make sure you are aware of the different levels and methods of tube feeding.

In its most basic form, tube feeding consists of simply giving you *glucose*—sugar—through an intravenous line. By doing that, physicians can usually manage to give you enough calories to keep your body from breaking down your own protein and fat—metabolically eating yourself up. But this will provide you with only a minimal supply of calories, and while it can be used to keep you alive for a prolonged period of time, you will begin to suffer nutritionally almost immediately.

In some ICUs, such as that in which the physician I quoted extensively practices, tube feeding is begun for most patients on admission, and the feeding is administered through a nasogastric tube. A mixture of foods from the "essential food groups" is then administered through the tube in liquid form. Assuming you do not pull the tube out, you can be fed this way for months at a time using the newer, very flexible, tubing available. However, even with the newest tubing this is a distinctly unpleasant experience, and it is not uncommon for patients to attempt to pull the tube out.

The next level of feeding, and an alternative to surgical insertion of a gastrostomy or *jejunostomy* tube, is the use of *total parenteral nutrition* (TPN). TPN is a relatively recent development and really is a modern medical miracle. A TPN patient is "fed" a liquid diet, consisting of elemental food products—proteins, fats, carbohydrates, vitamins, and minerals—in a liquid form that is delivered directly into the bloodstream through a vein. This makes it possible, for instance, for cancer patients who may not be able to take food by mouth, or patients who are unable to digest, to be nourished properly. While it is hardly a normal way to live, it is perfectly possible for patients on TPN to care for themselves for years and to lead relatively normal lives, other than the fact that they are feeding themselves or being fed by hooking a tube up to a vein in their arm or neck.

The most "invasive" method for providing nutrition to a patient is the insertion of either a gastrostomy tube or a jejunostomy tube. A gastrostomy tube is inserted surgically—through a hole cut in the abdomen—into the stomach; a jejunostomy tube is similarly inserted directly into the upper end of the small intestine. The placement of one of these tubes is a serious step in the care of a comatose or vegetative patient, as it involves surgery and represents a major commitment to the long-term maintenance of the patient. You should be *sure* to include a statement in your Living Will concerning your wishes about the use of these methods of feeding. This is a highly charged issue because your refusal to allow the insertion of a feeding tube is tantamount to demanding that you be "starved to death." You and your family may believe tube feeding is simply another technology that often is used inappropriately to maintain the physical existence of those who have long since ceased to live in *any* meaningful way. Many physicians, however, view the withdrawal of feeding as a final step they simply cannot take. So your representatives should be prepared for a court fight over this one—although courts are tending to decide in favor of decisions to stop feeding.

There are two final issues to be considered here: the first involves the use of *dialysis* to take over the function of the kidneys; the other is the question of Do Not Resuscitate (DNR), or No Code, orders.

Kidney dialysis is a potentially tremendously beneficial medical technology that maintains the lives—on a long-term basis—of about 60,000 persons in this country. The dialysis machine is used several times a week to remove impurities from the blood of patients whose kidneys have failed. At its best, dialysis allows these patients to lead relatively normal, productive, happy lives. There are dialysis patients who run major corporations, raise children, work in various occupations, attend school, and participate in all of life's normal activities. For some dialysis patients, however, life is a living hell of physical and psychological dependency on a machine. Life is so bleak for some, in fact, that the suicide rate among dialysis patients is about 400 times the national average.

Dialysis could be used for you in two distinct sets of circumstances. In one, you might be struggling with an acute illness, such as pneumonia, and your kidneys might shut down. Using dialysis for a few days, or weeks, might provide the kidneys with the break they need to recover their normal function, just as you would probably recover from the pneumonia. In the second case, you might be comatose, or vegetative, or in the last painful stages of cancer or congestive heart failure. As part of your dying process your kidneys might fail. An aggressive physician then might want to provide you with dialysis to keep you going. Were you fully conscious and competent, not only *might* you refuse dialysis under these circumstances but you would have the absolute *right* to do so—just as a competent individual has the right to refuse any medical treatment. Keep this in mind when you are preparing your Living Will.

The last question here involves the issuing of DNR, or No Code, orders. While the Intensive Care Unit director you met in the last chapter said he views DNR orders and Living Wills as separate issues, *you* should not. If you make it clear in your Living Will that you do *not* want to be resuscitated—and here we're talking about the chest pounding, paddle zapping "Code Blue" procedures you see in virtually every episode of every medical show on television—under certain circumstances, you will make it much easier for your relatives or the attorney who is seeing to your wishes. You may feel that if you are suffering from a terminal illness and have less than a given amount of time to live—give or take six months or a year—or if you are suffering from a debilitating illness such as Alzheimer's disease and are hospitalized, you would not want to be resuscitated should your heart stop. If that is the case, say so. Do not leave physicians and nurses to guess. Tell them what you want.

Four

THE WILLS
OF THE STATES

O_n the following pages, in alphabetical order, you will find copies of the Living Wills for each of the forty-one states and the District of Columbia that had a Living Will law as of October 1990. Each of these Living Wills either conforms precisely to the requirements of the state law where the law requires that a precise form be used or has been prepared by the attorneys for the Society for the Right to Die following the general guidelines of those states that allow some latitude in the preparation of your Living Will. In addition, you will find a form prepared by society attorneys for New Jersey and a Health Care Proxy form for New York. Although New Jersey doesn't yet have Living Will legislation, it has had extensive litigation on the subject, and the society's legal staff has prepared a form designed to conform with the requirements laid down in state court decisions.

It is recommended that you fill out, sign, and have properly witnessed one of these state forms whether or not you agree with all its limitations. That way, no one will be able to disregard your wishes using the argument that you failed to comply with the requirements of state law. If you do disagree with the restrictions of the official state form, *say so specifically* in both your written and videotaped Living Will— both of which you should prepare *in addition* to your official state form.

If you are a woman who has not yet gone through menopause, you should be aware that many state Living Will laws include clauses invalidating your Living Will should you be pregnant and terminally ill or comatose. Read your state's Living Will carefully. If it contains such a clause, and if you would not want your life sustained while in a persistent vegetative state and pregnant, *be sure you include such directions in a personal Living Will*. This is extremely important. Although there is no way to be sure whether your desires or those of the state would prevail in court, you can be sure that yours will *not* be recognized if you haven't stated them in writing.

If you have any questions regarding the Living Will law in your state, consult the Appendix to this book, your personal attorney, or your state attorney general's office.

ALABAMA

Declaration

Declaration made this _____ day of _____ (month, year).

I, _____ , being of sound mind, willfully and voluntarily make known my desires that my dying shall not be artificially prolonged under the circumstances set forth below, and do hereby declare:

If at any time I should have an incurable injury, disease, or illness certified to be a terminal condition by two physicians who have personally examined me, one of whom shall be my attending physician, and the physicians have determined that my death will occur whether or not life-sustaining procedures are utilized and where the application of life-sustaining procedures would serve only to artificially prolong the dying process, I direct that such procedures be withheld or withdrawn, and that I be permitted to die naturally with only the administration of medication or the performance of any medical procedure deemed necessary to provide me with comfort care.

[*Here you may insert any personalized directives.*]

In the absence of my ability to give directions regarding the use of such life-sustaining procedures, it is my intention that this declaration shall be honored by my family and physician(s) as the final expression of my legal right to refuse medical or surgical treatment and accept the consequences from such refusal.

I understand the full import of this declaration and I am emotionally and mentally competent to make this declaration.

Signed _____

City, County and Date of Residence,_____

_____

The declarant has been personally known to me and I believe him or her to be of sound mind. I did not sign the declarant's signature above for or at the direction of the declarant. I am not related to the declarant by blood or marriage, entitled to any portion of the estate of the declarant according to the laws of intestate succession or under any will or declarant or codicil thereto, or directly financially responsible for declarant's medical care.

Witness _____

ALASKA

Declaration

If I should have an incurable or irreversible condition that will cause my death within a relatively short time, it is my desire that my life not be prolonged by administration of life-sustaining procedures.

If my condition is terminal and I am unable to participate in decisions regarding my medical treatment, I direct my attending physician to withhold or withdraw procedures that merely prolong the dying process and are not necessary to my comfort or to alleviate pain.

I ( ) do ( ) do not desire that nutrition or hydration (food and water) be provided by gastric tube or intravenously if necessary.

Other directions:

Signed this _____ day of _____ (month, year).

Signature _____

Place _____

   The declarant is known to me and voluntarily signed or voluntarily directed another to sign this document in my presence.

Witness _____

Address _____

Witness _____

Address _____

State of _____

_____ Judicial District

The foregoing instrument was acknowledged before me

this _____ day of _____ , by

_____

Name of Person Who Acknowledged

_____

Signature of Person Taking Acknowledgment

_____

Title or Rank

_____

Serial Number, if any

This Declaration must be either witnessed by two persons or acknowledged by a person qualified to take acknowledgments under 09.63.010.

ARIZONA

Declaration

Declaration made this _____ day _____ (month, year).

I, _____ ,
being of sound mind, willfully and voluntarily make known
my desire that my dying not be artificially prolonged under
the circumstances set forth below and declare that:

If at any time I should have an incurable injury, disease
or illness certified to be a terminal condition by two
physicians who have personally examined me, one of
whom is my attending physician, and the physicians have
determined that my death will occur unless life-sustaining
procedures are used and if the application of life-sustaining
procedures would only serve to artificially prolong the dying
process, I direct that life-sustaining procedures be withheld
or withdrawn and that I be permitted to die naturally with
only the administration of medication, food or fluids or the
performance of medical procedures deemed necessary to
provide me with comfort care.

In the absence of my ability to give directions regarding
the use of life-sustaining procedures, it is my intention that
this declaration be honored by my family and attending
physician as the final expression of my legal right to refuse
medical or surgical treatment and accept the consequences
from such refusal.

I understand the full import of this declaration and I have
emotional and mental capacity to make this declaration.

Signed _____

City, County and State of Residence _____

The declarant is personally known to me and I believe him to be of sound mind.

Witness _____

Witness _____

ARKANSAS

"Terminal Condition"
Declaration

If I should have an incurable or irreversible condition that will cause my death within a relatively short time, and I am no longer able to make decisions regarding my medical treatment, I direct my attending physician, pursuant to the Arkansas Rights of the Terminally Ill or Permanently Unconscious Act, to withhold or withdraw treatment that only prolongs the process of dying and is not necessary to my comfort or to alleviate pain.

Other Directions:

_____

_____

I direct my attending physician to follow the instructions

of _____ ,

residing at _____ , as my Health Care Proxy, to make medical treatment decisions on my behalf consistent with my wishes.
[*If you don't wish to name a proxy, cross out this section.*]

_____

Signed this _____ day of _____ , 19 _____ .

Signature _____

Address _____

The declarant voluntarily signed this writing in my presence.

Witness _____

Address _____

Witness _____

Address _____

"Permanently Unconscious" Declaration

If I should become permanently unconscious, I direct my attending physician, pursuant to the Arkansas Rights of the Terminally Ill or Permanently Unconscious Act, to withhold or withdraw life-sustaining medical treatments that are no longer necessary to my comfort or to alleviate pain.

Other Directions:

_____

I direct my attending physician to follow the instructions

of _____ ,
residing at _____ , as
my Health Care Proxy, to make medical treatment decisions on my behalf consistent with my wishes.

[*If you don't wish to name a proxy, cross out this section.*]

_____

Signed this ____ day of _____ , 19 ____ .

Signature _____

Address _____

The declarant voluntarily signed this writing in my presence.

Witness _____

Address _____

Witness _____

Address _____

_____

CALIFORNIA

Directive to Physicians

Directive made this _____ day of _____ (month, year).

I, _____ ,
being of sound mind, willfully and voluntarily make known
my desire that my life shall not be artificially prolonged
under the circumstances set forth below, and do hereby
declare:

1. If at any time I should have an incurable injury, disease, or illness certified to be terminal by two physicians,
and where the application of life-sustaining procedures would
serve only to artificially prolong the moment of my death
and where my physician determines that my death is immi-

nent whether or not life-sustaining procedures are utilized, I direct that such procedures be withheld or withdrawn, and that I be permitted to die naturally.

2. In the absence of my ability to give directions regarding the use of such life-sustaining procedures, it is my intention that this directive shall be honored by my family and physician(s) as the final expression of my legal right to refuse medical or surgical treatment and accept the consequences from such refusal.

3. If I have been diagnosed as pregnant and that diagnosis is known to my physician, this directive shall have no force or effect during the course of my pregnancy.

4. I have been diagnosed at least 14 days ago as having a

terminal condition by _____ , M.D.,

whose address is _____ ,

and whose telephone number is _____ .

I understand that if I have not filled in the physician's name and address, it shall be presumed that I did not have a terminal condition when I made out this directive.

5. This directive shall have no force or effect five years from the date filled in above.

6. I understand the full import of this directive and I am emotionally and mentally competent to make this directive.

Signed _____

City, County and State of Residence _____

_____

The declarant has been personally known to me and I believe him or her to be of sound mind.

Witness _____

Witness _____

COLORADO

Declaration as to
Medical or Surgical Treatment

I, _____ ,
being of sound mind and at least eighteen years of age,
direct that my life shall not be artificially prolonged under
the circumstances set forth below and hereby declare
that:

1. If at any time my attending physician and one other
physician certify in writing that:

(a) I have an injury, disease, or illness which is not
curable or reversible and which, in their judgment, is a
terminal condition, and

(b) For a period of seven consecutive days or more, I
have been unconscious, comatose or otherwise incompetent so as to be unable to make or communicate responsible decisions concerning my person; then
I direct that life-sustaining procedures shall be withdrawn
and withheld persuant to the terms of this declaration, it
being understood that life-sustaining procedures shall not
include any medical procedure or intervention for nourishment or considered necessary by the attending physician to
provide comfort or alleviate pain. However, I may specifically direct, in accordance with Colorado law, that artificial
nourishment be withdrawn or withheld pursuant to the
terms of this declaration.

2. In the event that the only procedure I am being provided is artificial nourishment, I direct that one of the
following actions be taken:

(Initials of Declarant) a. Artificial nourishment shall not be
continued when it is the only procedure being provided;
or

(Initials of Declarant) b. Artificial nourishment shall be continued for _____ days when it is the only procedure being provided; or

(Initials of Declarant) c. Artificial nourishment shall be continued when it is the only procedure being provided.

3. I execute this declaration, as my free and voluntary act

this _____ day of _____ , 19____ .

By _____
              Declarant

The foregoing instrument was signed and declared by

_____ to be his declaration, in the presence of us, who, in his presence, in the presence of each other, and at his request, have signed our names below as witnesses, and we declare that, at the time of the execution of this instrument, the declarant, according to our best knowledge and belief, was of sound mind and under no constraint to undue influence.

Dated _____ , Colorado, this _____ day of

_____ , 19 ____ .

_____
                    Name and Address

_____
                    Name and Address

STATE OF COLORADO   )
)ss.
County of _____)

SUBSCRIBED and sworn before me by _____

_____ , and _____ ,

witnesses, as the voluntary act and deed of the declarant,

this _____ day of _____ , 19 ___ .
My commission expires:

_____
Notary Public

CONNECTICUT

If the time comes when I am incapacitated to the point when I can no longer actively take part in decisions for my own life, and am unable to direct my physician as to my own medical care I wish this statement to stand as a testament of my wishes.

I _____ (Name) request that I be allowed to die and not be kept alive through life support systems if my condition is deemed terminal. I do not intend any direct taking of my life, but only that my dying not be unreasonably prolonged. This request is made, after careful reflection, while I am of sound mind.

_____ (Signature)

_____ (Date)

_____ (Witness)

_____ (Witness)

DISTRICT OF COLUMBIA

Declaration

Declaration made this _____ day of _____
(month, year).

I, _____ ,
being of sound mind, willfully and voluntarily make known
my desires that my dying shall not be artificially prolonged
under the circumstances set forth below, and do declare:

If at any time I should have an incurable injury, disease or
illness certified to be a terminal condition by two (2) physicians who have personally examined me, one (1) of whom
shall be my attending physician, and the physicians have
determined that my death will occur whether or not life-
sustaining procedures are utilized and where the application of life-sustaining procedures would serve only to
artificially prolong the dying process, I direct that such
procedures be withheld or withdrawn, and that I be permitted to die naturally with only the administration of medication or the performance of any medical procedure deemed
necessary to provide me with comfort care or to alleviate
pain.

Other directions:

In the absence of my ability to give directions regarding
the use of such life-sustaining procedures, it is my intention that this declaration shall be honored by my family and
physician(s) as the final expression of my legal right to
refuse medical or surgical treatment and accept the consequences from such refusal.

I understand the full import of this declaration and am emotionally and mentally competent to make this declaration.

Signed _____

Address _____

I believe the declarant to be of sound mind. I did not sign the declarant's signature above for or at the direction of the declarant. I am at least eighteen (18) years of age and am not related to the declarant by blood or marriage, entitled to any portion of the estate of the declarant according to the laws of intestate succession of the District of Columbia or under any will of declarant or codicil thereto, or directly financially responsible for declarant's medical care. I am not the declarant's attending physician, an employee of the attending physician, or an employee of the health facility in which the declarant is a patient.

Witness_____

Witness_____

DELAWARE

Declaration

I, _____,
being an adult of sound mind, make this statement as a directive to be followed if I become unable to participate in decisions regarding my medical care.

If I should be in a terminal condition as confirmed in writing by two physicians, I direct my attending physician to withhold or withdraw medical maintenance treatment that will serve only to artificially prolong my dying. I further direct that treatment be limited to measures to keep me comfortable and relieve pain.

Other directions:

These directions express my legal right to refuse treatment. Therefore, I expect my family, doctors, and everyone concerned with my care to regard themselves as legally and morally bound to act in accord with my wishes, and in so doing be free of any legal liability for having followed my directions.

Date _____ Witness _____

Witness _____

Appointment of an Agent
[optional]

As provided in 2502 of the Delaware Death with Dignity

Act, I hereby appoint: _____ ,

who resides at: _____ ,

as my agent to act on my behalf if, owing to a condition resulting from illness or injury, I am deemed by my attending physician to be incapable of making a decision in the exercise of the right to accept or refuse medical treatment. This authorization includes the right to refuse medical treatment which would extend my life and the duty to act in good faith and with due regard for my benefits and interests.

Date _____ Signed _____

Witness _____

Witness _____

Witnesses' Attestation

I have read the provision of the law Del. Code Ann. tit. 16, 2503 (b) as reproduced below, and I am not prohibited from being a witness. I am over 18 years of age.

Date _____ Signed _____

Date _____ Signed _____

DELAWARE DEATH WITH DIGNITY ACT
Witnessing Subsection
16 Del. Code Ann. 2503 (b)

2503. Written Declaration.

(b) The declaration shall be signed by the declarant in the presence of two subscribing witnesses, neither of whom:

(1) is related to the declarant by blood or marriage;

(2) is entitled to any portion of the estate of the declarant under any will of the declarant or codicil thereto then existing nor, at the time of the declaration, is so entitled by operation of law then existing;

(3) has, at the time of the execution of the declaration, a present or inchoate claim against any portion of the estate of declarant;

(4) has a direct financial responsibility for the declarant's medical care; or

(5) is an employee of the hospital or other health care facility in which the declarant is a patient.

FLORIDA

Declaration

Declaration made this _____ day _____ (month, year).

I, _____ ,
willfully and voluntarily make known my desire that my dying shall not be prolonged under the circumstances set forth below, and I do hereby declare:

If at any time I should have a terminal condition and my attending physician has determined that there can be no recovery from such condition and my death is imminent, where the application of life-prolonging procedures would serve only to artificially prolong the dying process, I direct that such procedures be withheld or withdrawn, and that I be permitted to die naturally with only the administration of medication or the performance of any medical procedure deemed necessary to provide me with comfort care or to alleviate pain.

Other directions:

In the absence of my ability to give directions regarding the use of such life-prolonging procedures, it is my intention that this declaration shall be honored by my family and physician as the final expression of my legal right to refuse medical or surgical treatment and accept the consequences of such refusal.

If I have been diagnosed as pregnant and that diagnosis is known to my physician, this declaration shall have no force or effect during the course of my pregnancy.

I understand the full import of this declaration and I am emotionally and mentally competent to make this declaration.

Designation Clause
[*This section is optional*]

I authorize _____ ,

residing at _____ ,
to make treatment decisions on my behalf should I be (1)
diagnosed as suffering from a terminal condition and (2)
comatose, incompetent or otherwise mentally or physically
incapable of communication. I have discussed my desires
concerning terminal care with this person, and I trust his/
her judgment on my behalf. I understand that if I have not
filled in any name in this clause, my declaration will nevertheless be given effect should the appropriate circumstances
arise.

Signed _____

The declarant is known to me and I believe him or her to
be of sound mind.

Witness _____

Witness _____

GEORGIA

Living Will

Living will made this _____ day _____ (month, year).

I, _____ ,
being of sound mind, willfully and voluntarily make known
my desire that my life shall not be prolonged under the
circumstances set forth below and do declare:

1. If at any time I should have a terminal condition as
defined in and established in accordance with the proce-

dures set forth in paragraph (10) of Code Section 31-32-2 of the Official Code of Georgia Annotated, I direct that the application of life-sustaining procedures to my body be withheld or withdrawn and that I be permitted to die;

2. In the absence of my ability to give directions regarding the use of such life-sustaining procedures, it is my intention that this living will shall be honored by my family and physician(s) as the final expression of my legal right to refuse medical or surgical treatment and accept the consequences of such refusal;

Other instructions:

3. I understand that I may revoke this living will at any time;

4. I understand the full import of this living will, and I am at least 18 years of age and am emotionally and mentally competent to make this living will; and

5. If I am female and I have been diagnosed as pregnant, this living will shall have no force and effect during the course of my pregnancy.

Signed _____

City, County and State of Residence _____

_____

I hereby witness this living will and attest that:

(1) The declarant is personally known to me and I believe the declarant to be at least 18 years of age and of sound mind;

(2) I am at least 18 years of age;

(3) To the best of my knowledge, at the time of the execution of this living will, I:

(A) Am not related to the declarant by blood or marriage;

(B) Would not be entitled to any portion of the declarant's estate by any will or by operation of law under the rules of descent and distribution of this state;

(C) Am not the attending physician of declarant or any employee of the attending physician or an employee of the hospital or skilled nursing facility in which declarant is a patient;

(D) Am not directly responsible for the declarant's medical care; and

(E) Have no present claim against any portion of the estate of the declarant;

(4) Declarant has signed this document in my presence as above-instructed, on the date above first shown.

Witness _____ Witness _____

Address _____ Address _____

_____

Additional witness required when living will is signed in a hospital or skilled nursing facility.

I hereby witness this living will and attest that I believe the declarant to be of sound mind and to have made this living will willingly and voluntarily.

Witness _____

(Medical director of skilled nursing facility or staff physician not participating in the care of the patient, or chief of the hospital medical staff, or staff physician not participating in the care of the patient.)

HAWAII

Declaration

A. STATEMENT OF DECLARANT

Declaration made this _____ day of _____ (month, year).

I, _____ ,
being of sound mind, willfully and voluntarily make known my
desire that my dying shall not be artificially prolonged under
the circumstances set forth below, and do hereby declare:

If at any time I should have an incurable or irreversible
condition certified to be terminal by two physicians who
have personally examined me, one of whom shall be my
attending physician, and the physicians have determined
that I am unable to make decisions concerning my medical
treatment, and that without administration of life-sustaining
treatment my death will occur in a relatively short time, and
where the application of life-sustaining procedures would
only serve to prolong artificially the dying process, I direct
that such procedures be withheld or withdrawn, and that
I be permitted to die naturally with only the administration
of medication, nourishment, or fluids or the performance
of any medical procedure deemed necessary to provide me
with comfort or to alleviate pain.

Other directions:

In the absence of my ability to give directions regarding
the use of such life-sustaining procedures, it is my intention that this declaration shall be honored by my family and
physician(s) as the final expression of my legal right to refuse
medical or surgical treatment and accept the consequences
from such refusal.

I understand the full import of this declaration and I am emotionally and mentally competent to make this declaration.

Signed _____

Address _____

Statement of Witnesses

I am at least 18 years of age and
— not related to the declarant by blood, marriage or adoption; and
— not the attending physician, an employee of the attending physician, or an employee of the medical care facility in which the declarant is a patient.
The declarant is personally known to me and I believe the declarant to be of sound mind.

Witness _____

Address _____

Witness _____

Address _____

Notarization

Subscribed, sworn to and acknowledged before me by ____

_____ , the declarant,

and subscribed and sworn to before me by _____
_____ and _____ ,

witnesses, this _____ day of _____ , 19 ____ .

(SEAL)   Signed _____

_____

(official capacity of officer)

IDAHO

A Living Will

A Directive to Withhold or Provide Treatment

Directive made this _____ day _____ (month, year).

I, _____ ,
being of sound mind, willfully and voluntarily make known
my desire that my life shall not be artificially prolonged
under the circumstances below, do hereby declare that:

1. If at any time I should have an incurable injury, disease, illness or condition certified to be terminal by two medical doctors who have examined me, and where the application of life-sustaining procedures of any kind would serve only to prolong artificially the moment of my death, and where a medical doctor determines that my death is imminent, whether or not life-sustaining procedures are utilized, or I have been diagnosed as being in a persistent vegetative state, I direct that the following marked expression of my intent be followed and that I be permitted to die naturally, and that I receive any medical treatment or care that may be required to keep me free of pain or distress.

Check One Box

[ ] If at any time I should become unable to communicate my instructions, then I direct that all medical treatment, care, and nutrition and hydration necessary to restore my health, sustain my life, and to abolish or alleviate pain or distress be provided to me. Nutrition and hydration shall not be withheld or withdrawn from me if I would die from malnutrition or dehydration rather than from my injury, disease, illness or condition.

[ ] If at any time I should become unable to communicate my instructions and where the application of artificial

life-sustaining procedures shall serve only to prolong artificially the moment of my death, I direct such procedures be withheld or withdrawn except for the administration of nutrition and hydration.

[ ] If at any time I should become unable to communicate my instructions and where the application of artificial life-sustaining procedures shall serve only to prolong artificially the moment of my death, I direct such procedures be withheld or withdrawn including withdrawal of the administration of nutrition and hydration.

2. In the absence of my ability to give directions regarding the use of life-sustaining procedures, I hereby appoint

_____ (name)

currently residing at _____

_____ as my attorney-in-fact/proxy for making decisions relating to my health care in my place; and it is my intention that this appointment shall be honored by him/her, by my family, relatives, friends, physicians and lawyer as the final expression of my legal right to refuse medical or surgical treatment, and I accept the consequences of such a decision. I have duly executed a Durable Power of Attorney for health care decisions on this date.

3. In the absence of my ability to give further directions regarding my treatment, including life-sustaining procedures, it is my intention that this directive shall be honored by my family and physicians as the final expression of my legal right to refuse or accept medical and surgical treatment, and I accept the consequences of such refusal.

4. If I have been diagnosed as pregnant and that diagnosis is known to any interested person, this directive shall have no force during the course of my pregnancy.

5. I understand the full importance of this directive and am emotionally and mentally competent to make this directive. No participant in the making of this directive or in its being carried into effect, whether it be a medical doctor, my spouse, a relative, friend or any other person shall be held responsible in any way, legally, professionally, or socially, for complying with my directive.

Signed _____

City, county and state of residence _____

_____

The declarant has been known to me personally and I believe him/her to be of sound mind

Witness _____

Address _____

Witness _____

Address _____

ILLINOIS

Declaration

This declaration is made this _____ day of _____ (month, year).

I, _____ ,
being of sound mind, willfully and voluntarily make known my desires that my moment of death shall not be artificially postponed.

If at any time I should have an incurable and irreversible injury, disease or illness judged to be a terminal condition by my attending physician who has personally examined me and has determined that my death is imminent except for death delaying procedures, I direct that such procedures which would only prolong the dying process be withheld or withdrawn, and that I be permitted to die naturally with only the performance of any medical procedure deemed necessary by my attending physician to provide me with comfort care.

Other directions:

In the absence of my ability to give directions regarding the use of such death delaying procedures, it is my intention that this declaration shall be honored by my family and physician as the final expression of my legal right to refuse medical or surgical treatment and accept the consequences of such refusal.

Signed _____

City, County and State of Residence _____

_____

Attestation

The declarant has been personally known to me and I believe him or her to be of sound mind. I saw the declarant sign the declaration in my presence (or the declarant acknowledged in my presence that he had signed the declaration) and I signed the declaration as a witness in the presence of the declarant. I did not sign the declarant's signature above for or at the direction of the declarant. At the date of this instrument I am not entitled to any portion of the estate of the declarant according to the laws of intestate succession or, to the best of my knowledge and belief, under any will of declarant or other instrument taking effect at declarant's death, or directly financially responsible for declarant's medical care.

Witness _____

Address _____

Witness _____

Address _____

INDIANA

Living Will Declaration

Declaration made this _____ day _____ (month, year).

I, _____ ,
being at least eighteen (18) years old and of sound mind, willfully and voluntarily make known my desires that my dying shall not be artificially prolonged under the circumstances set forth below, and I declare:

If at any time I have an incurable injury, disease or illness certified in writing to be a terminal condition by my attending physician, and my attending physician has determined that my death will occur within a short period of time, and the use of life-prolonging procedures would serve only to artificially prolong the dying process, I direct that such procedures be withheld or withdrawn, and that I be permitted to die naturally with only the provision of appropriate nutrition and hydration and the administration of medication and the performance of any medical procedure necessary to provide me with comfort care or to alleviate pain.

In the absence of my ability to give directions regarding the use of life-prolonging procedures, it is my intention that this declaration be honored by my family and physician as the final expression of my legal right to refuse medical or surgical treatment and accept the consequences of the refusal.

I understand the full import of this declaration.

Signed _____

_____
City, County, and State of Residence

The declarant has been personally known to me, and I believe (him/her) to be of sound mind. I did not sign the declarant's signature for or at the direction of the declarant. I am not a parent, spouse or child of the declarant. I am not entitled to any part of the declarant's estate or directly financially responsible for the declarant's medical care. I am competent and at least eighteen (18) years old.

Witness _____ Date _____

Witness _____ Date _____

I O W A

Declaration

If I should have an incurable or irreversible condition that will cause my death within a relatively short time, it is my desire that my life not be prolonged by administration of life-sustaining procedures. If my condition is terminal and I am unable to participate in decisions regarding my medical treatment, I direct my attending physician to withhold or withdraw procedures that merely prolong the dying process and are not necessary to my comfort or freedom from pain.

Signed this _____ day of _____

Signature _____

City, County and State of Residence _____

_____

The declarant is known to me and voluntarily signed this document in my presence.

Witness _____

Address _____

Witness _____

Address _____

KANSAS

Declaration

Declaration made this _____ day _____ (month, year).

I, _____ ,
being of sound mind, willfully and voluntarily make known my desires that my dying shall not be artificially prolonged under the circumstances set forth below, and do hereby declare:

If at any time I should have an incurable injury, disease or illness certified to be a terminal condition by two physicians who have personally examined me, one of whom shall be my attending physician, and the physicians have determined that my death will occur whether or not life-sustaining procedures are utilized and where the application of life-sustaining procedures would serve only to artificially prolong the dying process, I direct that such procedures be withheld or withdrawn, and that I be permitted to die naturally with only the administration of medication or the performance of any medical procedure deemed necessary to provide me with comfort care.

In the absence of my ability to give directions regarding the use of such life-sustaining procedures, it is my intention that this declaration shall be honored by my family and physician(s) as the final expression of my legal right to refuse medical or surgical treatment and accept the consequences from such refusal.

I understand the full import of this declaration and I am emotionally and mentally competent to make this declaration.

Other Directions:

Signed _____

City, County and State of Residence _____

_____

The declarant has been personally known to me and I believe him or her to be of sound mind. I did not sign the declarant's signature above for or at the direction of the declarant. I am not related to the declarant by blood or marriage, entitled to any portion of the estate of the declarant according to the laws of intestate succession or under any will of declarant or codicil thereto, or directly financially responsible for the declarant's medical care.

Witness _____

Witness _____

KENTUCKY

Declaration

Declaration made this ＿＿ day of ＿＿＿＿＿ (month, year).

I, ＿＿＿＿＿＿＿＿＿＿＿＿＿＿＿＿＿＿＿＿＿＿＿ ,
willfully and voluntarily make known my desire that my dying
shall not be artificially prolonged under the circumstances
set forth below, and do hereby declare:

If at any time I should have a terminal condition and my
attending and one (1) other physician, in their discretion,
have determined such condition is incurable and irreversible
and will result in death within a relatively short time, and
where the application of life-prolonging treatment would serve
only to artificially prolong the dying process, I direct that
such treatment be withheld or withdrawn, and that I be permitted to die naturally with only the administration of medication or the performance of any medical treatment deemed
necessary to alleviate pain or for nutrition or hydration.

Other instructions:

In the absence of my ability to give directions regarding
the use of such life-prolonging treatment, it is my intention
that this declaration shall be honored by my attending
physician and my family as the final expression of my legal
right to refuse medical or surgical treatment, and I accept
the consequences of such refusal.

If I have been diagnosed as pregnant and that diagnosis is known to my attending physician, this directive

shall have no force or effect during the course of my pregnancy.

I understand the full import of this declaration and I am emotionally and mentally competent to make this declaration.

STATE OF KENTUCKY   )
) Sct.
COUNTY OF   )

Before me, the undersigned authority, on this day personally appeared _____,
Living Will Declarant, and _____
and _____,
known to me to be witnesses whose names are each signed to the foregoing instrument, and all these persons being first duly sworn, _____,
Living Will Declarant, declared to me and to the witnesses in my presence that the instrument is the Living Will Declaration of the Declarant and that the Declarant has willingly signed, and that such Declarant executed it as a free and voluntary act for the purposes therein expressed; and each of the witnesses stated to me, in the presence and hearing of the Living Will Declarant, that the declarant signed the Declaration as witness and to the best of such witness' knowledge, the Living Will Declarant was eighteen (18) years of age or over, of sound mind and under no constraint or undue influence.

Living Will Declarant: _____

Witness: _____

Address: _____

Witness: _____

Address: _____

Subscribed, sworn to and acknowledged before me by

_____,
Living Will Declarant, and subscribed and sworn to before

me by _____ and _____

_____, witnesses, on this the _____ day of _____
                                              (month, year)

Notary Public State at Large _____
Date my commission expires: _____

LOUISIANA

Declaration

Declaration made this day _____ day of _____ (month, year).
I, _____ ,
being of sound mind, willfully and voluntarily make known my
desire that my dying shall not be artificially prolonged under
the circumstances set forth below and do hereby declare:

If at any time I should have an incurable injury, disease, or
illness certified to be a terminal and irreversible condition
by two physicians who have personally examined me, one
of whom shall be my attending physician, and the physicians have determined that my death will occur whether or
not life-sustaining procedures are utilized and where the
application of life-sustaining procedures would serve only
to prolong artificially the dying process, I direct that such
procedures be withheld or withdrawn, and that I be permitted to die naturally with only the administration of medication or the performance of any medical procedures
deemed necessary to provide me with comfort care.

Other directions:

In the absence of my ability to give directions regarding the use of such life-sustaining procedures, it is my intention that this declaration shall be honored by my family and physician(s) as the final expression of my legal right to refuse medical or surgical treatment and accept the consequences from such refusal.

I understand the full import of this declaration and I am emotionally and mentally competent to make this declaration.

Designation Clause

[This section is optional]

I authorize _____ ,

residing at _____ ,
to make treatment decisions on my behalf should I be (1) diagnosed as suffering from a terminal condition and (2) comatose, incompetent or otherwise mentally or physically incapable of communication. I have discussed my desires concerning terminal care with this person, and I trust his/ her judgment on my behalf. I understand that if I have not filled in any name in this clause, my declaration will nevertheless be given effect should the appropriate circumstances arise.

Signed _____

City, Parish and State of Residence _____

_____

The declarant has been personally known to me and I believe him or her to be of sound mind.

Witness _____

Witness _____

MAINE

Declaration

If I should have an incurable or irreversible condition that will cause my death within a short time, and if I am unable to participate in decisions regarding my medical treatment, I direct my attending physician to withhold or withdraw procedures that merely prolong the dying process and are not necessary to my comfort or freedom from pain.

Signed this _____ day of _____ _____
         date   *month*   *year*

Signature _____

City, County and State of Residence _____
                                     city

_____
     county   *state*

The declarant is known to me and voluntarily signed this document in my presence.

Witness _____

Address _____

_____

Witness _____

Address _____

_____

MARYLAND

Declaration

If at any time I should have an incurable injury, disease, or illness certified to be a terminal condition by two (2) physicians who have personally examined me, one (1) of whom shall be my attending physician, and the physicians have determined that my death is imminent and will occur whether or not life-sustaining procedures are utilized and where the application of such procedures would serve only to artificially prolong the dying process, I direct that such procedures be withheld or withdrawn, and that I be permitted to die naturally with only the administration of medication, the administration of food and water, and the performance of any medical procedure that is necessary to provide comfort care or alleviate pain. In the absence of my ability to give directions regarding the use of such life-sustaining procedures, it is my intention that this declaration shall be honored by my family and physician(s) as the final expression of my right to control my medical care and treatment.

Declaration made this _____ day _____ (month, year).

I, _____ ,
being of sound mind, willfully and voluntarily direct that my dying shall not be artificially prolonged under the circumstances set forth in this declaration.

I am legally competent to make this declaration, and I understand its full import.

Signed _____

Address _____

Under penalty of perjury, we state that this declaration was signed by _____ in the presence of the undersigned who, at _____

_____

request, in _____
presence, and in the presence of each other, have hereunto signed our names and witness this _____
day of _____ , 19 _____ ,
and declare: The declarant is personally known to me, and
I believe the declarant to be of sound mind. I did not sign
the declarant's signature to this declaration. Based upon
information and belief, I am not related to the declarant by
blood or marriage, a creditor of the declarant, entitled to
any portion of the estate of the declarant under any existing
testamentary instrument of the declarant, entitled to any
financial benefit by reason of the death of the declarant, financially or otherwise responsible for the declarant's medical
care, or an employee of any such person or institution.

_____ Address _____

_____

_____ Address _____

_____

MINNESOTA

Health Care Declaration

Notice:

This is an important legal document. Before signing this
document, you should know these important facts:

(a) This document gives your health care provider or
your designated proxy the power and guidance to make

health care decisions according to your wishes when you are in a terminal condition and cannot do so. This document may include what kind of treatment you want or do not want and under what circumstances you want these decisions to be made. You may state where you want or do not want to receive any treatment.

(b) If you name a proxy in this document and that person agrees to serve as your proxy, that person has a duty to act consistently with your wishes. If the proxy does not know your wishes, the proxy has the duty to act in your best interests. If you do not name a proxy, your health care providers have a duty to act consistently with your instructions and/or tell you that they are unwilling to do so.

(c) This document will remain valid and in effect until and unless you amend or revoke it. Review this document periodically to make sure it continues to reflect your preferences. You may amend or revoke the declaration at any time by notifying your health care providers.

(d) Your named proxy has the same right as you have to examine your medical records and to consent to their disclosure for purposes relating to your health care or insurance unless you limit this right in this document.

(e) If there is anything in this document that you do not understand, you should ask for professional help to have it explained to you.

To My Family, Doctors and All Those Concerned with My Care

I, _____ ,
being an adult of sound mind, willfully and voluntarily make this statement as a directive to be followed if I am in a terminal condition and become unable to participate in decisions regarding my health care. I understand that my health care providers are legally bound to act consistently with my wishes, within the limits of reasonable medical

practice and other applicable law. I also understand that I have the right to make medical and health care decisions for myself as long as I am able to do so and to revoke this declaration at any time.

(1) The following are my feelings and wishes regarding my health care (you may state the circumstances under which this declaration applies):

(2) I particularly want to have all appropriate health care that will help in the following ways (you may give instructions for care you do want):

(3) I particularly do not want the following (you may list specific treatment you do not want in certain circumstances):

(4) I particularly want to have the following kinds of life-sustaining treatment if I am diagnosed to have a terminal condition (you may list the specific types of life-sustaining treatment you do want if you have a terminal condition):

(5) I particularly do not want the following kinds of life-sustaining treatment if I am diagnosed to have a terminal condition (you may list the specific types of life-sustaining treatment that you do not want if you have a terminal condition):

(6) I recognize that if I reject artificially administered sustenance, then I may die of dehydration or malnutrition rather than from my illness or injury. The following are my feelings and wishes regarding artificially administered sustenance should I have a terminal condition (you may indicate whether you wish to receive food and fluids given to you in some other way than by mouth if you have a terminal condition):

(7) Thoughts I feel are relevant to my instructions. (You may, but need not, give your religious beliefs, philosophy, or other personal values you feel are important. You may also state preferences concerning the location of your care.)

(8) PROXY DESIGNATION. (If you wish, you may name someone to see that your wishes are carried out, but you do not have to do this. You may also wish to name a proxy without including specific instructions regarding your care.

If you name a proxy you should discuss your wishes with that person.)

If I become unable to communicate my instructions, I designate the following person(s) to act on my behalf consistently with my instructions, if any, as stated in this document. Unless I write instructions that limit my proxy's authority, my proxy has full power and authority to make health care decisions for me. If a guardian or conservator of the person is to be appointed for me, I nominate my proxy named in this document to act as guardian or conservator of my person.

Name: _____

Address: _____

Phone Number: _____

Relationship: (If any) _____

If the person I have named above refuses or is unable to act on my behalf, or if I revoke that person's authority to act as my proxy, I authorize the following person to do so:

Name: _____

Address: _____

Phone Number: _____

Relationship: (If any) _____

I understand that I have the right to revoke the appointment of the person named above to act on my behalf at any time by communicating that decision to the proxy or to my health care provider.

DATE: _____

SIGNED: _____

STATE OF _____

COUNTY OF _____

Subscribed, sworn to, and acknowledged before me by

_____ on this _____

day of _____ , 19 _____

_____

NOTARY PUBLIC

OR

(Sign and date here in the presence of two adult witnesses, neither of whom is entitled to any part of your estate under a will or by operation of law, and neither of whom is your proxy.)

I certify that the declarant voluntarily signed this declaration in my presence and that the declarant is personally known to me. I am not named as a proxy by this declaration, and to the best of my knowledge, I am not entitled to any part of the estate of the declarant under a will or by operation of law.

Witness _____

Address _____

Witness _____

Address _____

Reminder: Keep the signed original with your personal papers. Give signed copies to your doctors, family, and proxy.

MISSISSIPPI

Declaration

Declaration made on _____ (date)

by _____ (name)

of _____ (address)

_____ (Social Security No.)

I, _____ ,
being of sound mind, declare that if any time I should
suffer a terminal physical condition which causes me severe distress or unconsciousness, and my physician, with
the concurrence of two (2) other physicians, believes that
there is no expectation of my regaining consciousness or a
state of health that is meaningful to me and but for the use
of life-sustaining mechanisms my death would be imminent,
I desire that the mechanisms be withdrawn so that I may
die naturally. However, if I have been diagnosed as pregnant
and that diagnosis is known to my physician, this declaration shall have no force or effect during the course of my
pregnancy. I further declare that this declaration shall be
honored by my family and my physician as the final expression of my desires concerning the manner in which I die.

Signed _____

I hereby witness this declaration and attest that:

(1) I personally know the Declarant and believe the Declarant to be of sound mind.

(2) To the best of my knowledge, at the time of the
execution of the declaration, I:

(a) Am not related to the Declarant by blood or
marriage.

(b) Do not have any claim on the estate of the Declarant.

(c) Am not entitled to any portion of the Declarant's estate by any will or by operation of law.

(d) Am not a physician attending the Declarant or a person employed by a physician attending the Declarant.

Witness _____

Address _____

_____ Soc. Sec. No. _____

Witness _____

Address _____

_____ Soc. Sec. No. _____

[*Mississippi law requires that, in order for this Will to be considered valid, a copy of it be mailed, along with a $10 filing fee, to:*

> *Division of Public Health Statistics*
> *P.O. Box 1700*
> *Jackson, MS 39215-1700*

In order to act on your Declaration your physician must receive a certified copy of it from the state Division of Public Health Statistics, along with a statement certifying that you have not filed a revocation with the department.]

MISSOURI

Declaration

I have the primary right to make my own decisions concerning treatment that might unduly prolong the dying process. By this declaration I express to my physician, family and friends my intent. If I should have a terminal condition it is my desire that my dying not be prolonged by administration of death-prolonging procedures. If my condition is terminal and I am unable to participate in decisions regarding my medical treatment, I direct my attending physician to withhold or withdraw medical procedures that merely prolong the dying process and are not necessary to my comfort or to alleviate pain. It is not my intent to authorize affirmative or deliberate acts or omissions to shorten my life rather only to permit the natural process of dying.

Signed this _____ day of _____

Signature _____

City, County and State of residence _____

_____

The declarant is known to me, is eighteen years of age or older, of sound mind and voluntarily signed this document in my presence.

Witness _____

Address _____

Witness _____

Address _____

Revocation Provision

I hereby revoke the above declaration.

Signed _____
(*Signature of Declarant*)

Date _____

MONTANA

Declaration

If I should have an incurable or irreversible condition that will cause my death within a relatively short time, it is my desire that my life not be prolonged by administration of life-sustaining procedures. If my condition is terminal and I am unable to participate in decisions regarding my medical treatment, I direct my attending physician to withhold or withdraw procedures that merely prolong the dying process and are not necessary to my comfort or freedom from pain. It is my intention that this declaration shall be valid until revoked by me.

Other instructions:

Signed this _____ day of _____ , _____ .

Signature _____

City, County and State of residence _____

_____

The declarant is known to me and voluntarily signed this document in my presence.

Witness _____

Address _____

Witness _____

Address _____

NEVADA

Directive to Physicians

I, _____ ,
being of sound mind, intentionally and voluntarily declare:

1. If at any time I am in a terminal condition and become comatose or am otherwise rendered incapable of communicating with my attending physician, and my death is imminent because of an incurable disease, illness or injury, I direct that life-sustaining procedures be withheld or withdrawn, and that I be permitted to die naturally.

2. It is my intention that this directive be honored by my family and attending physician as the final expression of my legal right to refuse medical or surgical treatment and to accept the consequences of my refusal.

3. If I have been found to be pregnant, and that fact is known to my physician, the directive is void during the course of my pregnancy.

I understand the full import of this directive, and I am emotionally and mentally competent to execute it.

Signed _____

City, County and State of Residence _____

_____

The declarant has been personally known to me and I believe _____

_____

to be of sound mind.

Witness _____

Witness _____

NEW HAMPSHIRE

Declaration

Declaration made this _____ day of _____ (month, year).

I, _____ ,
being of sound mind, willfully and voluntarily make known
my desire that my dying shall not be artificially prolonged
under the circumstances set forth below, do hereby declare:

If at any time I should have an incurable injury, disease,
or illness certified to be a terminal condition by 2 physicians who have personally examined me, one of whom
shall be my attending physician, and the physicians have
determined that my death will occur whether or not life-
sustaining procedures are utilized and where the application of life-sustaining procedures would serve only to
artificially prolong the dying process, I direct that such
procedures be withheld or withdrawn, and that I be permitted to die naturally with only the administration of medication, sustenance, or the performance of any medical
procedure deemed necessary to provide me with comfort
care.

In the absence of my ability to give directions regarding
the use of such life-sustaining procedures, it is my intention that this declaration shall be honored by my family and
physicians as the final expression of my right to refuse
medical or surgical treatment and accept the consequences
of such refusal.

I understand the full import of this declaration, and I am
emotionally and mentally competent to make this declaration.

Signed _____

State of _____

_____ County

We, the declarant and witnesses, being duly sworn each declare to the notary public or justice of the peace or other official signing below as follows:

1. The declarant signed the instrument as a free and voluntary act for the purposes expressed, or expressly directed another to sign it for him.

2. Each witness signed at the request of the declarant, in his presence, and in the presence of the other witness.

3. To the best of my knowledge, at the time of the signing the declarant was at least 18 years of age, and was sane of mind and under no constraint or undue influence.

_____ Declarant

_____ Witness

_____ Witness

The affidavit shall be made before a notary public or justice of the peace or other official authorized to administer oaths in the place of execution, who shall not also serve as a witness, and who shall complete and sign a certificate in content and form substantially as follows:

Sworn to and signed before me by _____ ,

declarant, _____

and _____ , witness,

on _____ .

_____
Signature

_____
Official Capacity

NEW JERSEY

Medical Power of Attorney

I, _____ , residing

at _____ ,

as principal, hereby designate and appoint _____

_____ , residing at _____

_____ ,

as my agent for all matters relating to my health care including, but not limited to, full power to give, or refuse or revoke consent to all medical, surgical and hospital care. Specifically, I authorize my agent to order the refusal, discontinuation or withdrawal of all forms of life-sustaining treatment if my agent determines that based upon his/her knowledge of my personal instructions, beliefs, and value system I would not want to have such treatment instituted or continued. This power of attorney shall not be affected by any disability of the principal.

Signed, sealed and
delivered in the presence
of:

_____

Agent's signature   *Principal's signature*

STATE OF NEW JERSEY   )
) ss.:
COUNTY OF   )

BE IT REMEMBERED THAT ON THIS _____ day of _____

19 _____ , before me the subscriber, a Notary Public of New

Jersey, personally appeared _____
who I am satisfied is the person named in and who executed the within Power of Attorney and he/she acknowledged
that he/she signed, sealed and delivered said Power of
Attorney as his/her voluntary act and deed, for the uses and
purposes therein expressed.

_____
Notary Public

NEW MEXICO

Declaration

Declaration made this _____ day of _____ (month, year).

I, _____ ,
being of sound mind, willfully and voluntarily make known
my desire that my dying shall not be artificially prolonged
under the circumstances set forth below, and do hereby
declare:

If at any time I should be terminally ill or injured, or in an
irreversible coma, as certified by two physicians, and where
the application of maintenance medical treatment would
serve only to futilely prolong my dying, and where the
certifying physicians determine that my death will occur
whether or not maintenance medical treatment is utilized, I

direct that such treatment be withheld or withdrawn and that I be permitted to die.

Other directions:

In the absence of my ability to give directions regarding the use of such maintenance medical treatment, it is my intention that this declaration shall be honored by my family and physician(s) as the final expression of my legal right to refuse medical or surgical treatment, and I accept the consequences of such refusal.

I understand the full import of this declaration and I am emotionally and mentally competent to make this declaration.

Attestation Clause

This document, consisting of _____ pages, this page included, was this _____ day _____ , 19 _____ , signed by _____
in the State of New Mexico, pursuant to the Right to Die Act, in the presence of us who at his/her request and in his/her presence, and in the presence of each other, have signed our names as witnesses. We believe the declarant has reached the age of majority and is of sound mind at the time of this signing.

Witness _____

Residing at _____

Witness _____

Residing at _____

Subscribed, sworn to and acknowledged before me by

_____ , the Declarant, and

_____ and

_____ , witnesses,

this _____ day _____ , 19 _____ .

_____
Notary Public

NEW YORK

New York State Health Care Proxy Form

[Author's note: The following is the suggested form prepared to comply with the requirements of New York's Health Care Proxy law. The Health Care Proxy is similar to a Durable Power of Attorney (see page 116). I would suggest that, in addition to filling out this form in detail, especially concerning your wishes regarding artificial nutrition and hydration—food and water—you also prepare both written and videotaped Living Wills, which you should give to your Health Care Proxy.]

I, _____ , hereby appoint

(name, home address and telephone numbers) _____

_____

_____

as my health care agent to make any and all health care decisions for me, unless I specify otherwise in this document.

This health care proxy shall take effect at such time as I am no longer able to make my own health care decisions.

[Author's note: If you have any specific instructions that would limit your proxy's authority in any way, you must do so in writing. Unless you specify that you would, or would not, want artificial nutrition and hydration—tube feeding and water—your agent will not be legally authorized to make decisions regarding its use.]

SPECIFIC INSTRUCTIONS: [Should you choose to make any.]

_____

_____

_____

_____

_____

_____

I direct my agent to make health care decisions in accordance with my wishes and instructions as stated above or otherwise known to him or her. I also direct my agent to abide by any limitations on his or her authority as stated above or as otherwise known to him or her.

In the event the person I appoint is unable, unwilling or unavailable to act as my agent, I hereby appoint (name, home address and telephone number of alternate agent)

_____

_____

I understand that unless I specifically revoke it, or choose to include an expiration date below, this proxy shall remain in effect from this day forward.

Date of Expiration of this proxy

[OPTIONAL]: _____

My Signature: _____

My Address: _____

Today's Date: _____

THE TWO WITNESSES WHO ARE SIGNING BELOW DECLARE that the person who signed, or asked someone to sign this proxy on his or her behalf, is known to me and appears to be of sound mind and acting of his or her free will. He or she signed this document, or asked someone to sign it for him or her, in my presence. I am not the person appointed by this document to act as proxy.

Witness: _____

Address: _____

Witness: _____

Address: _____

NORTH CAROLINA

Declaration of
a Desire for a Natural Death

I, _____ ,
being of sound mind, desire that my life not be prolonged by extraordinary means if my condition is determined to be terminal and incurable. I am aware and understand that this writing authorizes a physician to withhold or discontinue extraordinary means.
  Other directions:

This the _____ day of _____ , _____ .

Signature _____

I hereby state that the declarant, _____

_____ ,
being of sound mind signed the above declaration in my
presence and that I am not related to the declarant by
blood or marriage and that I do not know or have a
reasonable expectation that I would be entitled to any
portion of the estate of the declarant under any existing
will or codicil of the declarant or as an heir under the
Intestate Succession Act if the declarant died on this
date without a will. I also state that I am not the declarant's attending physician or an employee of the declarant's
attending physician, or an employee of a health facility
in which the declarant is a patient or an employee of a
nursing home or any group-care home where the declarant
resides. I further state that I do not now have any claim
against the declarant.

Witness _____

Witness _____

[*In order for this document to be legally valid in the state
of North Carolina it must be sworn to before a state Superior Court clerk or a North Carolina notary public.*]

Certificate

I, _____ ,
Clerk (assistant Clerk) of Superior Court or Notary Public
(circle one as appropriate) for _____

County hereby certify that _____ ,
the declarant, appeared before me and swore to me and to
the witnesses in my presence that this instrument is his
Declaration of a Desire for a Natural Death, and that he
had willingly and voluntarily made and executed it as his
free act and deed for the purpose expressed in it.

I further certify that _____

and _____ ,
witnesses, appeared before me and swore that they witnessed

_____ ,
declarant, sign the attached declaration, believing him to
be of sound mind; and also swore that at the time they
witnessed the declaration (i) they were not related within
the third degree to the declarant or to the declarant's
spouse, and (ii) they did not know or have a reasonable
expectation that they would be entitled to any portion of
the estate of the declarant upon the declarant's death under any will of the declarant or codicil thereto then existing
or under the Intestate Succession Act as it provides at that
time, and (iii) they were not a physician attending the
declarant or an employee of an attending physician or an
employee of a health care facility in which the declarant
was a patient or an employee of a nursing home or any
group-care home in which the declarant is a resident, and
(iv) they did not have a claim against declarant. I further
certify that I am satisfied as to the genuineness and due execution of the declaration.

This _____ day _____ , _____
Clerk (Assistant Clerk) or Superior Court of Notary Public
(circle one as appropriate) for the County of _____

NORTH DAKOTA

Declaration

Declaration made this _____ day of _____ (month, year).

I, _____ ,
being at least eighteen years of age and of sound mind,
willfully and voluntarily make known my desire that my life
must not be artificially prolonged under the circumstances
set forth below, do hereby declare:

1. If at any time I should have an incurable condition caused
by injury, disease or illness certified to be a terminal condition by two physicians, and where the application of life-
prolonging treatment would serve only to artificially prolong
the process of my dying and my attending physician determines that my death is imminent whether or not life-
prolonging treatment is utilized, I direct that such treatment
be withheld or withdrawn, and that I be permitted to die
naturally.

2. In the absence of my ability to give directions regarding
the use of such life-prolonging treatment, it is my intention
that this declaration be honored by my family and physicians as the final expression of my legal right to refuse
medical or surgical treatment and accept the consequences
of that refusal, which is death.

3. If I have been diagnosed as pregnant and that diagnosis
is known to my physician, this declaration is not effective
during the course of my pregnancy.

4. I understand the full import of this declaration and I am
emotionally and mentally competent to make this declaration.

5. I understand that I may revoke this declaration at any
time.

          Signed _____

City, County, and State of Residence _____

_____

The declarant has been personally known to me and I believe the declarant to be of sound mind. I am not related to the declarant by blood or marriage, nor would I be entitled to any portion of the declarant's estate upon the declarant's death. I am not the declarant's attending physician, a person who has a claim against any portion of the declarant's estate upon the declarant's death, or a person financially responsible for the declarant's medical care.

Witness _____

Witness _____

O K L A H O M A

Directive to Physicians

Directive made this _____ day of _____ (month, year).

I,_____ ,
being of sound mind and twenty-one (21) years of age or older, willfully and voluntarily make known my desire that my life shall not be artificially prolonged under the circumstances set forth below, and do hereby declare:

(1) If at any time I should have an incurable irreversible condition caused by injury, disease, or illness certified to be a terminal condition by two physicians, I direct that life-sustaining procedures be withheld or withdrawn and that I be permitted to die naturally, if the application of life-sustaining procedures would serve only to artificially prolong the moment of my death and my attending physician determines that my death is imminent whether or not life-sustaining procedures are utilized;

Other directions:

(2) In the absence of my ability to give directions regarding the use of such life-sustaining procedures, it is my intention that this directive shall be honored by my family and physicians as the final expression of my legal right to refuse medical or surgical treatment and accept the consequences of such refusal;

(3) If I have been diagnosed as pregnant and that diagnosis is known to my physician, this directive shall have no force or effect during the course of my pregnancy;

(4) I have been diagnosed and notified as having a terminal condition by_____ , M.D. or D.O.,

whose address is _____

and whose telephone number is _____ .

I understand that if I have not filled in the name and address of the physician, it shall be presumed that I did not have a terminal condition when I made out this directive;

(5) This directive shall be in effect until it is revoked;

(6) I understand the full import of this directive and am emotionally and mentally competent to make this directive; and

(7) I understand that I may revoke this directive at any time.

Signed _____

City, County and State of Residence _____

_____ .

The declarant has been personally known to me and I believe said declarant to be of sound mind. I am twenty-one (21) years of age or older, I am not related to the declarant by blood or marriage, nor would I be entitled to any portion of the estate of the declarant upon the death of said declarant, nor am I the attending physician of the declarant or any employee of the attending physician or a health care facility in which the declarant is a patient, or a patient in the health care facility in which the declarant is a patient, nor am I financially responsible for the medical care of the declarant, or any person who has a claim against any portion of the estate of the declarant upon the death of the declarant.

Witness _____

Witness _____
State of Oklahoma

County of _____
Before me, the undersigned authority, on this day person-

ally appeared _____

_____ (declarant),

_____ (witness)
whose names are subscribed to the foregoing instrument in their respective capacities, and, all of said persons being by me duly sworn, the declarant declared to me and to the said witnesses in my presence that said instrument is his or her "Directive to Physicians," and that the declarant had willingly and voluntarily made and executed it as the free act and deed of the declarant for the purposes therein expressed.

The foregoing instrument was acknowledged before me

this _____ day of _____ , 19 ____ .

Signed _____

Notary Public in and for _____ County, Oklahoma

My Commission Expires _____ day of _____, 19 _____ .

OREGON

Directive to Physicians

Directive made this _____ day _____ (month, year).

I, _____ ,
being of sound mind, willfully and voluntarily make known
my desire that my life shall not be artificially prolonged
under the circumstances set forth below and do hereby
declare:

1. If at any time I should have an incurable injury,
disease or illness certified to be a terminal condition by
two physicians, one of whom is the attending physician,
and where the application of life-sustaining procedures
would serve only to artificially prolong the moment of
my death and where my physician determines that my
death is imminent whether or not life-sustaining procedures are utilized, I direct that such procedures be
withheld or withdrawn, and that I be permitted to die
naturally.

2. In the absence of my ability to give directions regarding the use of such life-sustaining procedures, it is my
intention that this directive shall be honored by my family
and physician(s) as the final expression of my legal right to
refuse medical or surgical treatment and accept the consequences from such refusal.

3. I understand the full import of this directive and I am
emotionally and mentally competent to make this directive.

Signed _____

Signed _____

City, County and State of Residence _____

_____

I hereby witness this directive and attest that:

(1) I personally know the Declarant and believe the Declarant to be of sound mind.

(2) To the best of my knowledge, at the time of the execution of this directive, I:

(a) Am not related to the Declarant by blood or marriage,

(b) Do not have any claim on the estate of the Declarant,

(c) Am not entitled to any portion of the Declarant's estate by any will or by operation of law, and

(d) Am not the physician attending the Declarant or a person employed by a physician attending the Declarant or a person employed by a health facility in which the Declarant is a patient.

(3) I understand that if I have not witnessed this directive in good faith I may be responsible for any damages that arise out of giving this directive its intended effect.

Witness _____

Witness _____

SOUTH CAROLINA

Declaration
of a Desire for a
Natural Death

State of South Carolina,

County of _____

I, _____ ,

a resident of and domiciled in the City of _____ ,
County of _____ , State of South Carolina, make this
Declaration this _____ day of _____ , 19 _____ .
I willfully and voluntarily make known my desire that no

life-sustaining procedures be used to prolong my dying if my condition is terminal, and I do hereby declare:

If at any time I have an incurable injury, disease or illness certified to be a terminal condition by two physicians who have personally examined me, one of whom is my attending physician, and the physicians have determined that my death will occur without the use of life-sustaining procedures and where the application of life-sustaining procedures would serve only to prolong the dying process, I direct that such procedures be withheld or withdrawn, and that I be permitted to die naturally with only the administration of medication or the performance of any medical procedure necessary to provide me with comfort care.

Other directions:

In the absence of my ability to give directions regarding the use of such life-sustaining procedures, it is my intention that this Declaration be honored by my family and physicians as the final expression of my legal right to refuse medical or surgical treatment and I accept the consequences from such refusal.

I am aware that this Declaration authorizes a physician to withhold or withdraw life-sustaining procedures. I am emotionally and mentally competent to make this Declaration.

This Declaration may be revoked by the declarant, without regard to his physical or mental condition.

(1) By being defaced, torn, obliterated, or otherwise destroyed by the declarant or by some person in the presence of and by the direction of the declarant.

(2) By a written revocation signed and dated by the declarant expressing his or her intent to revoke. The revocation shall become effective only upon communica-

tion to the attending physician by the declarant or by a person acting on behalf of the declarant. The attending physician shall record in the patient's medical record the time and date when he received notification of the written revocation.

(3) By a verbal expression by the declarant of his intent to revoke the declaration. The revocation shall become effective only upon communication to the attending physician by the declarant. The attending physician shall record in the patient's medical record the time, date and place of the revocation and the time, date, and place, if different, of when he received notification of the revocation.

_____
Declarant

Affidavit

State of _____

County of _____

We, _____ ,

_____ and

_____ ,

the witnesses whose names are signed to the foregoing

Declaration, dated the _____ day of _____ , 19 ____ ,
being first duly sworn, do hereby declare to the undersigned authority that the declaration was on that date signed by the said declarant as and for his *Declaration of a Desire for a Natural Death* in our presence and we, at his request and in his presence, and in the presence of each other, did thereunto subscribe our names as witnesses on that date. The declarant is personally known to us and we believe him to be of sound mind. None of us is disqualified as a witness to this Declaration by any provision of the South

Carolina Death With Dignity Act. None of us is related to the declarant by blood or marriage; nor directly financially responsible for the declarant's medical care; nor entitled to any portion of the declarant's estate upon his decease, whether under any will or as an heir by intestate succession; nor the beneficiary of a life insurance policy of the declarant; nor the declarant's attending physician; nor an employee of such attending physician; nor a person who has claim against the declarant's decedent's estate as of this time. No more than one of us is an employee of a health facility in which the declarant is a patient. If the declarant is a patient in a hospital or skilled or intermediate care nursing facility at the date of execution of this declaration at least one of us is an ombudsman designated by the State Ombudsman, Office of the Governor.

Witness _____

Witness _____

Witness _____

Subscribed, sworn to, and acknowledged before me by ___

_____ the declarant,

and subscribed and sworn to before me by _____

_____

and _____ , the witnesses,

this _____ day of _____ , 19 ___ .

_____

Notary Public for

My commission expires: _____
SEAL

TENNESSEE

Living Will

I, _____ ,
willfully and voluntarily make known my desire that my
dying shall not be artificially prolonged under the circumstances set forth below and do hereby declare:

If at any time I should have a terminal condition and my
attending physician has determined that there can be no
recovery from such condition and my death is imminent,
where the application of life-prolonging procedures would
serve only to artificially prolong the dying process, I direct
that such procedures be withheld or withdrawn, and that I
be permitted to die naturally with only the administration
of medications or the performance of any medical procedure deemed necessary to provide me with comfortable
care or to alleviate pain. In the absence of my ability to give
directions regarding the use of such life-prolonging procedures, it is my intention that this declaration shall be honored by my family and physician as the final expression of
my legal right to refuse medical or surgical treatment and
accept the consequences of such refusal.

Other instructions:

I understand fully the import of this declaration and I am
emotionally and mentally competent to make this declaration. In acknowledgment whereof, I do hereinafter affix

my signature on this _____

day of _____ , 19 _____ .

_____
Declarant

We, the subscribing witnesses hereto, are personally acquainted with and subscribe our names hereto at the request of the declarant, an adult, whom we believe to be of sound mind, fully aware of the action taken herein and its possible consequences.

We the undersigned witnesses further declare that we are not related to the declarant by blood or marriage; that we are not entitled to any portion of the estate of the declarant upon his/her decease under any will or codicil thereto presently existing or by operation of law then existing that we are not the attending physician, an employee of the attending physician or a health facility in which the declarant is a patient; and that we are not a person who, at the present time, has a claim against any portion of the estate of the declarant upon his/her death.

_____
Witness

_____
Witness

Subscribed, sworn to and acknowledged before me by ____

_____ , the declarant,

and subscribed and sworn to before me by _____

_____

and _____ , witnesses,

this _____ day of _____ , 19 _____ .

_____
Notary Public

TEXAS

Directive to Physicians

Directive made this _____ day of _____ (month, year).

I, _____ , being of sound mind, willfully and voluntarily make known my desire that my life shall not be artificially prolonged under the circumstances set forth below, and do hereby declare:

1. If at any time I should have an incurable condition caused by injury, disease, or illness certified to be a terminal condition by two physicians, and where the application of life-sustaining procedures would serve only to artificially prolong the moment of my death and where my attending physician determines that my death is imminent or will result within a relatively short time without application of life-sustaining procedures, I direct that such procedures be withheld or withdrawn and that I be permitted to die naturally.

2. In the absence of my ability to give directions regarding the use of life-sustaining procedures, it is my intention that this directive shall be honored by my family and physicians as the final expression of my legal right to refuse medical or surgical treatment and accept the consequences from such refusal.

Other directions:

3. If I have been diagnosed as pregnant and that diagnosis is known to my physician, this directive shall have no force or effect during the course of my pregnancy.

4. This directive shall be in effect until it is revoked.
5. I understand the full import of this directive and I am emotionally and mentally competent to make this directive.
6. I understand that I may revoke this directive at any time.

Signed _____

City, County, and State of Residence _____

_____

I am not related to the declarant by blood or marriage; nor would I be entitled to any portion of the declarant's estate on his/her decease; nor am I the attending physician of the declarant or an employee of the attending physician; nor am I a patient in the health care facility in which the declarant is a patient, or any person who has a claim against any portion of the estate of the declarant upon his/her decease. Furthermore, if I am an employee of a health facility in which the declarant is a patient, I am not involved in providing direct patient care to the declarant nor am I directly involved in the financial affairs of the health facility.

Witness _____

Witness _____

UTAH

Directive to Physicians and Providers of Medical Services
(Pursuant to Section 75-1104, UCA)

This directive is made this _____ day of _____, _____ .

1. I, _____ ,
being of sound mind, willfully and voluntarily make known

my desire that my life not be artificially prolonged by life-sustaining procedures except as I may otherwise provide in this directive.

2. I declare that if at any time I should have an injury, disease, or illness, which is certified in writing to be a terminal condition by two physicians who have personally examined me, and in the opinion of those physicians the application of life-sustaining procedures would serve only to unnaturally prolong the moment of my death and to unnaturally postpone or prolong the dying process, I direct that these procedures be withheld or withdrawn and my death be permitted to occur naturally.

3. I expressly intend this directive to be a final expression of my legal right to refuse medical or surgical treatment and to accept the consequences from this refusal which shall remain in effect notwithstanding my future inability to give current medical directions to treating physicians and other providers of medical services.

4. I understand that the term "life-sustaining procedures" does not include the administration of medication or sustenance, or the performance of any medical procedure deemed necessary to provide comfort care, or to alleviate pain, except to the extent I specify below that any of these procedures be considered life-sustaining:

[Author's note: At this point in the Utah will you may insert any specific directions you have regarding particular types of care or treatment you might not want under certain circumstances. For instance, you might say that you would not, in accordance with the principles of the American Medical Association, want to be tube fed if you were diagnosed as being in a persistent vegetative state.]

5. I reserve the right to give current medical directions to physicians and other providers of medical services so long as I am able, even though these directions may conflict with the above written directive that life-sustaining procedures be withheld or withdrawn.

6. I understand the full import of this directive and declare that I am emotionally and mentally competent to make this directive.

_____

Declarant's Signature

_____

City, County and State of Residence

We witnesses certify that each of us is 18 years of age or older and each personally witnessed the declarant sign or direct the signing of this directive; that we are acquainted with declarant and believe him to be of sound mind; that the declarant's desires are as expressed above; that neither of us is a person who signed the above directive on behalf of the declarant; that we are not related to the declarant by blood or marriage nor are we entitled to any portion of declarant's estate according to the laws of intestate succession of this state or under any will or codicil of declarant; that we are not directly financially responsible for declarant's medical care; and that we are not agents of any health care facility in which declarant may be a patient at the time of signing this directive.

_____   _____

Signature of Witness   *Signature of Witness*

_____   _____

Address of Witness   *Address of Witness*

VERMONT

Terminal Care Document

To my family, my physician, my lawyer, my clergyman. To any medical facility in whose care I happen to be. To any individual who may become responsible for my health, welfare or affairs.

Death is as much a reality as birth, growth, maturity and old age—it is the one certainty of life. If the time comes when

I, _____ ,
can no longer take part in the decision of my own future, let this statement stand as an expression of my wishes, while I am still of sound mind. If the situation should arise in which I am in a terminal state and there is no reasonable expectation of my recovery, I direct that I be allowed to die a natural death and that my life not be prolonged by extraordinary measures. I do, however, ask that medication be mercifully administered to me to alleviate suffering even though this may shorten my remaining life.

Other directions:

This statement is made after careful consideration and is in accordance with my strong convictions and beliefs. I want the wishes and directions here expressed carried out to the extent permitted by law. Insofar as they are not legally enforceable, I hope that those to whom this will is addressed will regard themselves as morally bound by these provisions.

Signed _____

Date: _____

Witness _____

Witness _____

Copies of this request have been given to: _____

_____

_____

_____

VIRGINIA

Declaration

Declaration made this _____ day _____ (month, year).

I, _____ , willfully and voluntarily make known my desire and do hereby declare:

Choose Only One of the Next Two Paragraphs and Cross Through the Other

If at any time I should have a terminal condition and my attending physician has determined that there can be no recovery from such condition, my death is imminent, and I am comatose, incompetent or otherwise mentally or physically incapable of communication, I designate _____ to make a decision on my behalf as to whether life-prolonging procedures should be withheld or withdrawn, I wish to be permitted to die naturally with only the administration of medication or the performance of any medical procedures deemed necessary to provide me with comfort care or to alleviate pain.

Or

If at any time I should have a terminal condition and my attending physician has determined that there can be no recovery from such condition and my death is imminent, where the application of life-prolonging procedures would serve only to artificially prolong the dying process, I direct that such procedures be withheld or withdrawn, and that I be permitted to die naturally with only the administration of medication or the performance of any medical procedures deemed necessary to provide me with comfort care or to alleviate pain.

Other directions:

In the absence of my ability to give directions regarding the use of such life-sustaining procedures, it is my intention that this declaration shall be honored by my family and physician as the final expression of my legal right to refuse medical or surgical treatment and accept the consequences of such refusal.

I understand the full import of this declaration and I am emotionally and mentally competent to make this declaration.

Signed _____

The declarant is known to me and I believe him or her to be of sound mind.

Witness _____

Witness _____

WASHINGTON

Directive to Physicians

Directive made this _____ day _____ (month, year).

I, _____ , being of sound mind, willfully and voluntarily make known my desire that my life shall not be artificially prolonged under the circumstances set forth below, and do hereby declare that:

(a) If at any time I should have an incurable injury, disease, or illness certified to be a terminal condition by two physicians, and where the application of life-sustaining procedures would serve only to artificially prolong the moment of my death and where my physician determines that my death is imminent whether or not life-sustaining procedures are utilized, I direct that such procedures be withheld or withdrawn, and that I be permitted to die naturally.

(b) In the absence of my ability to give directions regarding the use of such life-sustaining procedures, it is my intention that this directive shall be honored by my family and physician(s) as the final expression of my legal right to refuse medical or surgical treatment and I accept the consequences from such refusal.

(c) If I have been diagnosed as pregnant and that diagnosis is known to my physician, this directive shall have no force or effect during the course of my pregnancy.

(d) I understand the full import of this directive and I am emotionally and mentally competent to make this directive:

Other directions:

Signed _____

City, County and State of Residence _____

_____

The declarer has been personally known to me and I believe him or her to be of sound mind.

Witness _____

Witness _____

WEST VIRGINIA

Declaration

Declaration made this _____ day of _____ (month, year).

I, _____ ,
being of sound mind, willfully and voluntarily make known my desires that my dying shall not be artificially prolonged under the circumstances set forth below, and do declare:

If at any time I should have an incurable injury, disease, or illness certified to be a terminal condition by two physicians who have personally examined me, one of whom is my attending physician, and the physicians have determined that my death will occur whether or not life-sustaining procedures are utilized and where the application of life-sustaining procedures would serve only to artificially prolong the dying process, I direct that such procedures be withheld or withdrawn, and that I be permitted to die naturally with only the administration of nutrition, medication or the performance of any medical procedure deemed necessary to provide me with comfort care or to alleviate pain.

In the absence of my ability to give directions regarding the use of such life-sustaining procedures, it is my intention that this declaration be honored by my family and physician(s) as the final expression of my legal right to refuse medical or surgical treatment and accept the consequences resulting from such refusal.

I understand the full import of this declaration and I am emotionally and mentally competent to make this declaration.

Signed _____

Address _____

_____

_____

I did not sign the declarant's signature above for or at the direction of the declarant. I am at least eighteen years of age and am not related to the declarant by blood or marriage, entitled to any portion of the estate of the declarant according to the laws of intestate succession of the state of West Virginia or to the best of my knowledge under any will of declarant or codicil thereto, or directly financially responsible for the declarant's medical care. I am not the declarant's attending physician, an employee of the attending physician, or an employee of the health facility in which the declarant is a patient.

Witness _____

Witness _____

State of _____ , County of _____

_____

WISCONSIN

Declaration to Physicians

Declaration made this _____ day of _____ (month, year).

1. I, _____ ,
being of sound mind, willfully and voluntarily state my
desire that my dying may not be artificially prolonged if I
have an incurable injury or illness certified to be a terminal
condition by 2 physicians who have personally examined
me, one of whom is my attending physician, and if the
physicians have determined that my death is imminent, so
that the application of life-sustaining procedures would
serve only to prolong artificially the dying process. Under
these circumstances, I direct that life-sustaining procedures
be withheld or withdrawn and that I be permitted to die
naturally, with only:

a. The continuation of nutritional support and fluid maintenance; and

b. The alleviation of pain by administering medication or
other medical procedure.

Other instructions:

2. If I am unable to give directions regarding the use of
life-sustaining procedures, I intend that my family and physician honor this declaration as the final expression of my
legal right to refuse medical or surgical treatment and to
accept the consequences from this refusal.

3. If I have been diagnosed as pregnant and the physician
knows of this diagnosis, this declaration has no effect during the course of my pregnancy.

4. This declaration takes effect immediately.

I understand this declaration and I am emotionally and mentally competent to make this declaration.

Signed _____

Address _____

I know the declarant personally and I believe him or her to be of sound mind. I am not related to the declarant by blood or marriage, and am not entitled to any portion of the declarant's estate under any will of declarant. I am neither the declarant's attending physician, the attending nurse, the attending medical staff, nor an employee of the attending physician or of the inpatient health care facility in which the declarant may be a patient and I have no claim against the declarant's estate at this time, except that I am not a health care provider who is involved in the medical care of the declarant, I may be an employee of the inpatient health care facility regardless of whether or not the facility may have a claim against the estate of the declarant.

Witness _____

Witness _____

WYOMING

Declaration

Declaration made this _____ day of _____

_____ (month, year), I, _____

_____ , being of sound mind, willfully and voluntarily make known my desire that my dying shall not be artificially prolonged under the circumstances set forth below, do hereby declare:

If at any time I should have an incurable injury, disease or other illness certified to be a terminal condition by two (2) physicians who have personally examined me, one (1) of whom shall be my attending physician, and the physicians have determined that my death will occur whether or not life-sustaining procedures are utilized and where the application of life-sustaining procedures would serve only to artificially prolong the dying process, I direct that such procedures be withheld or withdrawn, and that I be permitted to die naturally with only the administration of medication or the performance of any medical procedure deemed necessary to provide me with comfort care.

Other directions:

If, in spite of this declaration, I am comatose or otherwise unable to make treatment decisions for myself, **I HEREBY** designate

_____ to make treatment decisions for me.

In the absence of my ability to give directions regarding the use of life-sustaining procedures, it is my intention that this declaration shall be honored by my family and physician(s) and agent as the final expression of my legal right to refuse medical or surgical treatment and accept the consequences from this refusal. I understand the full import of this declaration and I am emotionally and mentally competent to make this declaration.

Signed _____

City, County and State of Residence _____

_____

The declarant has been personally known to me and I believe him or her to be of sound mind. I did not sign the declarant's signature above for or at the direction of the declarant. I am not related to the declarant by blood or marriage, entitled to any portion of the estate of the declarant or codicil thereto, or directly financially responsible for the declarant's medical care.

Witness _____

Witness _____

Five

WRITING YOUR
LIVING WILL

Once you have filled out a Living Will according to the law of your state—assuming that your state has a law governing Living Wills—you have four or more things to do to protect yourself as best you can from eternal medical intrusion: You *must* prepare a very personal Living Will; you *should* prepare a *durable power of attorney;* you *should* prepare a videotaped Living Will; and you *must* make sure that copies of these documents are preserved in places where your attorney, physician, and next of kin have access to them. First, let us deal with the question of how to prepare a durable power of attorney.

The President's Commission for the Study of Ethical Problems in Medicine and Biomedical and Behavioral Research described a power of attorney as a document "by which one person (the 'principal') confers upon another person (the 'agent') the legally recognized authority to perform certain acts on the principal's behalf. For instance, a person who moves to a new city and who leaves behind an automobile for someone else to sell can execute a power of attorney to permit an agent to complete the necessary legal documents for the sale. . . . Powers of attorney may also be general, conferring authority on the agent to act on behalf of the principal in all matters. Such actions by agents are as legally binding on principals as if the latter had performed the acts themselves. . . . Using (power of attorney), a person can nominate another to make health care decisions if he or she becomes unable to make those decisions."

While standard powers of attorney are terminated in the event the principal becomes incapacitated—which, as the commission points out, is "precisely the point at which it is needed"—more than forty states have now passed laws allowing for durable power of attorney. By preparing a durable power of attorney, you appoint a person to act on your behalf to exercise your right to make decisions concerning your medical treatment and to exercise your absolute right to refuse treatment. The following durable power of attorney is included in the Delaware Death with Dignity Act. By all means, fill it out. Then, if you have any questions regarding its applicability in your state, consult with your attorney or contact Concern for Dying / Society for the Right to Die, which is listed in the Appendix of this book.

Durable Power of Attorney

I hereby appoint _____ , who

resides at _____ , as my agent to act on my behalf if, owing to a condition resulting from illness or injury, I am deemed by my attending physician to be incapable of making a decision in the exercise of the right to accept or refuse medical treatment. This authorization includes the right to refuse medical treatment which

would extend my life and the duty to act in good faith and with due regard for my benefits and interests.

Date _____ Signed_____

Witness _____

Witness _____

Witnesses' Attestation

I am not related to _____
by blood or marriage. I am not entitled to any portion of his or her estate, either by any existing will or codicil thereto, or by existing state law. I have no present or inchoate claim against any portion of his or her estate. I have no direct financial responsibility for his or her medical care and I am not employed by any physician caring for him or her nor by any health care facility in which he or she resides.

(cross out either inappropriate personal pronoun)

Date _____ Signed _____

Date _____ Signed _____

As you learned when you read what Dr. Nicholas Benjamin (chapter 2) has to say about withdrawing life supports, it is absolutely essential that whoever reads your Living Will is convinced that you prepared it in an informed and knowing basis, rather than on a whim. You want to convince the reader of the will that you have thought long and hard about what life and death mean to you, and the circumstances in which death would be more desirable than life. You must convince your physicians—and you may well have to convince a judge—that you prepared the will *knowing* that you could not possibly consider all the possible configurations of every medical disaster that might befall you. You are simply

making your treatment decisions—they are not *requests*—as best they can be made in advance, and you are prepared to die as a result of those decisions.

The distinction between decisions and requests is an important one. Many physicians, including many of those sympathetic to the concept of Living Wills, view the document as the vehicle by which you are making advance *requests* regarding your final medical treatment. That is not what your will is or should be. Your Living Will is, in effect, your written responses to choices your physician might give you could you respond. "Mr. Smith," your physician might say, "we have a few options left. We could try another course of antibiotics to see if we can get on top of this infection, and we could put in a gastrostomy tube to enable us to increase your nutritional intake. Now . . ."

At that point, your Living Will interrupts your physician, just as you might if you were conscious and competent, to say, in effect, "Stop right there, doctor. I've thought long and hard about this, and I do not want anything more done. No antibiotics. No tube feeding. I just want you to use whatever painkillers you need to make me comfortable, and let it go at that."

"But Mr. Smith, if we do not attempt these treatments you will die. I feel I have to do these things."

"Doctor," you might say, "I refuse permission. If you attempt to treat me in this manner you are doing so against my will, and I will ask my attorney to file criminal charges of assault and battery against you. And I will also refuse to pay for any treatment forced on me against my will."

It is unlikely that you would ever have the nerve to say such things to your physician. You might also feel that one of the problems in our society today is our incredible degree of litigiousness. And you would be right on both counts. However, your Living Will allows you to say in writing things that you might feel but probably would never say to someone in person. As to the question of our being overly

litigious, the reason we have too many suits is that people view lawsuits, including medical malpractice suits, as a wooden horse from which they can grab the brass ring. That's not what we're talking about here. What you would be doing by threatening the filing of criminal assault charges, or threatening to have your proxy file suit for damages, is using the threat of legal action, or legal action itself, to protect your legal rights. You would not be looking to get rich. Rather, you would be doing your best to ensure that you are not taken advantage of by a healthcare system that, in effect, has you as prisoner.

The states' forms in the previous chapter should provide you with a rough idea of how you might write your Living Will. As this is a personal statement on your part, you should use your own words. No one can write this for you. To give you some guidance, however, I am including three more wills here. The first and second are prepared and distributed by Concern for Dying / Society for the Right to Die. The third is my own Living Will, which I include as an example of what a personal statement might be.

When you are reading these three Living Wills, you will note a major difference between them and *all* the state forms. While the state forms are all based on the assumption that you have a right to refuse life-sustaining treatment if you are suffering from a terminal condition, the wills prepared by Concern for Dying / Society for the Right to Die and my Living Will are simply based on the premise that anyone has an absolute right to refuse medical treatment. Period. There is no need to discuss terminal illness unless you want to. You can refuse any and all medical treatment, whether you are terminally ill or are suffering from a common cold. This right has been held to be absolute. Unless the state can prove to a court that the state has an overwhelming interest in preserving your life—as, for instance, in the case of an otherwise healthy young single mother of three children whose children would become wards of the state if she refused a life-preserving blood transfusion—you cannot be treated against your will. So simply include in your Living Will those conditions under which *you* would not want to be treated.

LIVING WILL DECLARATION

[Prepared by the Society for the Right to Die]

To My Family, Doctors, and All Those Concerned with My Care:

I, _____ ,
being of sound mind, make this statement as a directive to be followed if I become unable to participate in decisions regarding my medical care.

If I should be in an incurable or irreversible mental or physical condition with no reasonable expectation of recovery, I direct my attending physician to withhold or withdraw treatment that merely prolongs my dying. I further direct that treatment be limited to measures to keep me comfortable and to relieve pain.

These directions express my legal right to refuse treatment. Therefore I expect my family, doctors, and everyone concerned with my care to regard themselves as legally and morally bound to act in accord with my wishes, and in so doing to be free of any legal liability for having followed my directions.

I especially do not want: _____

_____

_____

_____

_____

_____

Other instructions/comments: _____

_____

_____

_____

_____

_____

_____

Proxy Designation Clause: Should I become unable to communicate my instructions as stated above, I designate the
following person to act in my behalf:

Name _____

Address _____
If the person I have named above is unable to act in my
behalf, I authorize the following person to do so:

Name _____

Address _____
[*The Proxy Designation Clause is an optional addition to
your Living Will. The will itself is, in effect, your proxy, but
you may use the Proxy Designation to name a particular
individual to see to it that your wishes are carried out.*]

Signed _____

Date: _____

Witness _____

Witness _____

Keep the signed original with your personal papers at home. Give signed copies to your doctors, family, and to your proxy.

Before we move on to the will prepared by Concern for Dying, we should consider the question of just who should be given copies of your will. In addition to the suggestions of the Society for the Right to Die, I would add the following:

1. Concern for Dying / Society for the Right to Die (see the Appendix for the address) has an excellent program whereby, in exchange for a $25 contribution, they will keep a copy of your Living Will in their master file. You can then carry a card in your wallet informing any emergency medical personnel that you have a Living Will and where copies of it may be found.

2. In exchange for a $10 membership fee, the group will send you a wallet-size Living Will.

3. In addition to giving signed copies of your Living Will to your family members, attorney, and physician, you should also have a copy placed in your bank safe deposit box along with the other papers there, and, if you are a nursing home resident, have a copy given to the director of the nursing home in which you reside. In addition, if you are considering residence in a nursing home, carefully discuss the question of Living Wills with the administration *before* you move in. In at least one recent "right-to-die" court case, some nursing home personnel testified that they do not honor Living Wills under any circumstances. If that is the case in a nursing home you are considering for yourself or a member of your family, find it out ahead of time.

4. If you have a chronic, debilitating condition, such as ALS, Alzheimer's, or chronic obstructive pulmonary disease (COPD), and would not want to be resuscitated should you suffer cardiac arrest and be rushed to a hospital emergency room, have the words *Do Not Resuscitate* engraved on the sort

of medical alert wrist bracelet you can purchase in many pharmacies. On the back of the bracelet place the message: *Living Will: Call,* and place the phone number of your next of kin, physician, or attorney.

Furthermore, if you are suffering from a chronic condition and there are only a few hospitals in your community, you might go to the director of each hospital's emergency room, introduce yourself, explain your situation, and leave a copy of your Living Will with the emergency room director. You may or may not find the director willing to accommodate you, but if she refuses your request, you might tell her that you are writing a letter to your attorney, informing her of your conversation at the hospital and asking her to file criminal assault charges against the emergency room director if you are later resuscitated in her facility.

If you are already in a hospital or nursing home, *demand* that a copy of your Living Will be made a permanent part of your medical record.

MY LIVING WILL
TO MY FAMILY, MY PHYSICIAN, MY LAWYER, AND ALL OTHERS WHOM IT MAY CONCERN
[Prepared by Concern for Dying]

Death is as much a reality as birth, growth, maturity, and old age—it is the one certainty of life. If the time comes when I can no longer take part in decisions for my own future, let this statement stand as an expression of my wishes and directions, while I am still of sound mind.

If at such a time the situation should arise in which there is no reasonable expectation of my recovery from extreme physical or mental disability, I direct that I be allowed to die and not be kept alive by medications, artificial means, or "heroic measures." I do, however, ask that medication be mercifully administered to me to alleviate suffering even though this may shorten my remaining life.

This statement is made after careful consideration and is in accordance with my strong convictions and beliefs. I want the wishes and directions here expressed carried out to the extent permitted by law. Insofar as they are not legally enforceable, I hope that those to whom this will is addressed will regard themselves as morally bound by these provisions.

[*Optional specific provisions to be made in this space.*]

DURABLE POWER OF ATTORNEY [*optional*]

I hereby designate _____
to serve as my attorney-in-fact for the purpose of making medical treatment decisions. This power of attorney shall remain effective in the event that I become incompetent or otherwise unable to make such decisions for myself.

Signed _____

Date: _____

Witness _____

_____
Address

Witness _____

_____
Address

Optional Notarization:

Sworn and subscribed to before me this _____ day of _____ ,

19 _____ .

_____
Notary Public (seal)

Copies of this request have been given to _____

_____

[Optional] My Living Will is registered
with Concern for Dying / Society for the Right to Die
[No.____]

DURABLE POWER OF ATTORNEY
FOR DESIGNATION OF HEALTH CARE AGENT

KNOW ALL PERSONS BY THESE PRESENT, that I, _____

_____

of _____ ,
　　　　City　　　　　　　County　　　　　　　State

do hereby constitute and appoint _____
　　　　　　　　　　　　　　　　　　　　Name

_____　_____
　　　　Address　　　　　　　　　　　Telephone

as my attorney for me and in my name to make health care
decisions for me. For the purposes of this document, "health
care decision" means consent, refusal to consent, or withdrawal of consent to any care, treatment, service, or procedure to maintain, diagnose, or treat an individual's physical
or mental condition.

In the event _____ is unable or unwilling
to act, I hereby constitute and appoint _____
　　　　　　　　　　　　　　　　　　　　　　　　Name

_____　_____
　　　　Address　　　　　　　　　　　Telephone

to be such attorney for me.

**Statement of Desires, Special Provisions,
and Limitations**

_____

_____

_____

The person designated above is given authority to inspect
and disclose any information relating to my physical and
mental health, and is authorized to sign documents, waiv-
ers, and releases, including documents titled or purporting
to be a "Refusal to Permit Treatment" and "Leaving the
Hospital Against Medical Advice" and to execute any waiver
or release from liability required by a hospital or physician.

I declare this power of attorney shall not be affected by
my disability or incapacity, and that the authority granted
herein shall continue during any period while I am disabled
or incapacitated.

IN WITNESS WHEREOF, I have hereunto set my hand and
seal this

_____ day of _____, 19 _____

_____
Signature

_____   _____
Witness Signature   Address of Witness

_____   _____
Witness Signature   Address of Witness

Subscribed and sworn to before me on this _____ day of
_____ 19 _____ .

_____
Notary Public

AUTHOR'S LIVING WILL

Now we come to my Living Will. Obviously, you will not want to copy what I write. My Living Will is my personal statement regarding what I want for myself under certain circumstances, should they ever arise. My feelings and beliefs may be very different from yours, and I do not want to influence you in any way. You may, however, find reading my Living Will useful in that it will provide you with an example of how you might prepare your own personal statement.

INSTRUCTIONS REGARDING THE USE OF MEDICAL TECHNOLOGIES TO SUSTAIN THE LIFE OF B. D. COLEN

To my attending physicians, primary care nurse, family members, and attorney:

I am writing this statement for two reasons: Should I need medical intervention to maintain my life and be unable to discuss that intervention with you, this statement will speak for me. Additionally, should I need such medical care *and* am still able to communicate rationally with you, I want you to view this statement as a prior expression of my views on these issues and thus as proof that, should I refuse treatment while conscious and rational, I am acting on long held, well thought out beliefs.

As a medical writer I am a believer in the wonders of modern medicine. I believe the development of antibiotics, tube feeding of all sorts and varieties, the invention and refinement of the ventilator, the refinement of kidney dialysis, and other blessings of modern medical technology have saved and greatly improved the lives of countless millions. At the same time, however, having covered the cases of Karen Ann Quinlan and Nancy Ellen Jobes, as well as many similar cases, I am aware that this technology is a double-edged sword: We must be as willing to refrain from using it as we are willing to use it, lest it come to control, rather than improve, our lives.

I have often written over the years, and fervently believe, that the physician who plays God is not the physician who turns off a respirator or withdraws any other life-sustaining technology. After all, the physician who "gives up" is simply acknowledging the limits of medicine and of his human abilities, and is withdrawing human technology in order to allow a natural process—dying—to conclude. No, the physician who plays God is the physician who turns on the respirator in the first place, interrupting a natural process, or the physician who refuses to acknowledge "defeat" in the vain belief that he can fend off death forever. I, for one, do not ever want to become the victim of such a physician.

With this in mind, let me say that I can think of no therapy—short of the implantation of an artificial heart—that I would not undergo as a short-term bridge to health. I would be willing to be on a respirator, to be tube fed, or to be dialyzed. I would only, however, be willing to have these therapies used as acute, rather than chronic, treatment. If I am placed on a respirator in the belief that within a matter of a few days I will be strong enough to be removed from the machine, and you then find that I cannot be weaned from the respirator, I want the respirator turned off. I do not want to live my life as an appendage of a machine. While some might be willing to live that way, I would not be.

If I should suffer a stroke or some other form of medical accident that affects my motor control or ability to communicate, I do not want to live if I do not *at least* have control of my hands and full mental acuity. I believe I could adjust to losing my ability to walk, as well as my ability to speak. I would not, however, want to live if I were unable to fully control my hands and thus engage in certain activities, such as physically interacting with my children, model-making, photography, writing, and playing the guitar, which give me both pleasure and a sense of purpose.

I understand that some period of assessment may be necessary in order for my attending physicians to have a reasonable idea of how far I might be able to recover following a stroke or accident. However, I do not want that understanding used as an excuse for those same physicians to evade their responsibility to provide me with the kind of care I am requesting. I do not want them to wait so long to conclude an assessment that I awake some day to find that I am paralyzed from the neck down and unable to make any decisions for myself at that point.

Therefore, if after a reasonable but brief period of assessment, my attending physicians, in consultation with appropriate specialists, decide that recovery of the use of my hands is unlikely and/or if those same physicians conclude that my mental faculties will be impaired, I hereby order them to withdraw any medical treatment being used to sustain my life, specifically including, but not limited to, the use of the respirator, antibiotics, dialysis, and the provision of nutrition.

Similarly, should I be suffering from a debilitating illness, such as cancer, and be beyond any reasonable hope of recovery, I want all life-supporting therapies discontinued.

Additionally, if at any time I am diagnosed as being in a persistent vegetative state or am in a coma of more than six weeks' duration, I want all life-supporting therapies withdrawn.

I want it clearly understood that, under the circumstances I have outlined, I am refusing permission for any medical treatment that is not specifically and solely intended to keep me comfortable while I die. I do not wish to be in pain and am sophisticated enough to know that there is no need for me to suffer pain, even if nutrition is stopped—I understand that it may be necessary for my comfort, as well as for the psychological comfort of my family and the members of the medical staff caring for me, to continue hydration.

If the medical staff caring for me, or the administrators of the institution in which I am being cared for, refuse to honor this directive and insist on treating me against my will, I will consider such treatment an act of criminal assault, and want my proxy to file a criminal assault and battery complaint against those involved in this violation of my basic right to refuse medical treatment. Additionally, I want my family members to file a multi-million dollar civil damage suit against those involved in treating me against my will. I believe we are far too litigious a society, and that the fear of litigation is having a chilling effect upon the traditional doctor-patient relationship. However, if the threat of litigation is the only language those treating me understand, then that is the language in which I want them addressed.

I have prepared this statement of my wishes fully aware of its implications. I want it understood by my next of kin that any physician or other care giver acting upon my requests as outlined here is acting on my behalf, and should be considered free from all civil liability.

Finally, I want to thank anyone who helps to fulfill my wishes for the courage they show in doing so and the faithfulness those physicians involved show to the injunction to, "first of all, do no harm."

Signed _____
B. D. Colen

Date _____

Witness _____

Witness _____

Six

PREPARING YOUR VIDEOTAPED LIVING WILL

Once you have completed your personal written Living Will and filled out your state's Living Will—if you live in a state with a Living Will law—it's time to get out the video camera to prepare your videotaped Living Will. Before you dismiss the idea of making one, let me point out that if your family has to go into court to protect your right to refuse life-sustaining medical treatment, a videotape of you voicing your refusal is the best piece of evidence their attorney could possibly present on your behalf. Time after time in so-called right-to-die court cases, judges have bemoaned the fact that they had no way to know what the comatose or vegetative principal in the case *really* wanted. The best way for you to tell a judge or, for that matter, Intensive Care Unit director, hospital administrator, or attorney what you *really* want is to do just that: Make a videotape in which you carefully spell out just what kind of treatment you would or would not want and under what circumstances you would or wouldn't want it.

"But I don't even own a VCR, let alone a video camera," you say. No problem. If you don't have a video camera the odds are that a member of your family, a friend, or a neighbor has one you could borrow. And, if all else fails, the equipment can be rented, relatively inexpensively, from many large photo equipment and VCR dealers.

So how do you go about this project? First, ask a member of your family—your spouse, one of your parents, or an adult child—a close friend, or your clergyman or attorney to help you with this project. You are going to want this other person to sit with you "on camera" and discuss your statement with you.

Once you have someone to help you, purchase a top-of-the-line blank videotape. This is not the time to scrimp. A high-quality tape is going to give you truer color renditions under less than optimum lighting conditions and is likely to remain viewable for far longer than a bargain tape.

With your equipment in hand, choose the right setting. Pick a comfortable, well-lit spot in your house or apartment. Do you have a favorite chair in the den or living room? A kitchen table at which you like to sit enjoying a cup of coffee with a friend each day? Pick a setting in which you can be comfortable and relaxed, but also be sure to pick one in which there will be sufficient light on your face to make a clear, sharp videotape.

Then, position the video camera on a tripod, and set the zoom lens—which virtually all video cameras and camcorders have these days—so that both you and the person with whom you will be talking are in the picture. Ask your helper to sit in your chair and count to 10 in a normal voice while you make a test tape. Play that tape back to make sure that you—and the other chair—can be seen, that the sound is sufficiently loud so that you can be understood easily when speaking in a normal voice, and that the light is sufficient. If the room isn't bright enough and turning on lights and opening shades doesn't provide sufficient light, try another setting.

One last thing before you begin. If your video camera has a device that allows you to imprint the time and date on the videotape or if it has a frame counter, use it. If the camera doesn't have that capability, then make sure that a working clock is easily visible in the picture. The idea here is to make it clear to viewers of your videotaped Living Will that no one could have tampered with the tape.

All right, now you're ready to begin. With your friend or family member sitting in one chair facing the camera, turn the camera on and sit down in the second chair. Then turn back toward the camera and introduce yourself.

What follows here is a script you can use for guidance. Do not attempt to follow this script word for word. Rather, follow its form. Word things in a manner that feels comfortable to you—but make sure that you include on your tape all the important points you made in your written Living Will:

Mary Jones. I'm Mary Jones, and this is my daughter, Inga Hanson. It's two P.M., October 17, 1990. I've asked Inga to join me here this afternoon to discuss my thoughts and wishes about the use of life-prolonging medical technology. I am making this videotaped Living Will to supplement my written Living Will, of which my husband, John Jones, Inga, and my attorney, Robert Wiggins, all have copies.

Inga Hanson. Mother, why do you think it's necessary for us to tape this?

Mary Jones. Because I don't want anyone to have any questions about my right to refuse medical treatment if I'm unable to speak for myself. I don't want some doctor or judge saying that he doesn't know if I knew what I really wanted. I don't want them to say I was confused, or upset, or senile, or anything else. Do I seem senile to you? [*Mary asks this, looking directly at the camera, as Inga laughs.*]

Inga Hanson. But why do you think you need this, Mother? George and I know what you want and we'll tell your doctors. Besides, we all have copies of your Living Will.

Mary Jones. I know that, Inga, and I know that you'll do what you can. But I've read about enough of these court cases in the newspapers to know that you need all the help you can get these days. In the *Quinlan* case, and then the *Brophy* case and the *Jobes* case, family members all knew what those people wanted, but look at what they had to go through anyway. I just want to make all this easier for you and Dad and everyone else.

Inga Hanson. When did you first think you needed a Living Will?

Mary Jones. I guess I first thought about it last March, after I was hospitalized for that gallbladder surgery. I hated feeling dependent, confined to that hospital bed. It may sound funny to you, but I realized I'd rather die than live that way. I've had a full life, and you know how important my freedom has always been to me. I wouldn't want to live for a minute if I thought I'd be a burden to Dad or any of you children. And life wouldn't be worth living to me if all I could do was lie in a bed, being taken care of by somebody else.

Inga Hanson. But mother, we all grow old someday. We'd still love you even if you couldn't do the things you do now. You'd never be a burden to us.

Mary Jones. The question, dear, is whether I'd think I was a burden. And I would. And if I thought that, I wouldn't want to live. I don't want to be kept alive if I can't be independent. If I can't at least wash and dress myself, make my own meals, and leave wherever I'm living for at least part of the day, then I wouldn't want to be kept alive. I don't have anything against medical machinery, these respirators and such, but I don't want to live with one for longer than it would take me to get better and go home if I was sick.

Inga Hanson. So, what you're saying is that it would be all right with you if a respirator were used if you had, umm, pneumonia, let's say, and had to be on the machine for a few days, but then got better and went home?

Mary Jones. That's right. But I wouldn't want to be kept alive by a respirator, or fed by tube, or use one of those kidney machines for any long period of time. If I'm sick, either I want to get better or die. Period.

Inga Hanson. But Mother, what if you have a stroke and you're partially paralyzed?

Mary Jones. I already told you: If I can't care for myself, I want care stopped. All care. If I get pneumonia under those circumstances, I don't want antibiotics. If I have a heart attack, I don't want them bringing me back. I just want to be allowed to die when my time comes, not when some doctor decides it's my time.

Inga Hanson. Well you know, Mother, the doctor might say that it's one thing for you to sit here now, at age sixty-three, in perfect health, and say these things, but you might feel a whole lot differently under other circumstances.

Mary Jones. That's why we're making this tape. [*Here Mary Jones turns directly toward the camera and looks it right in the lens.*]

Doctor, or Judge, or whomever I'm talking to, you don't know me and I don't know you. But let me assure you that I know myself. I know how I would and would not want to live, and you don't. I know what life means to me, and you don't. And that's why I'm telling you now, after thinking about it a great deal, that I don't want anything done to keep me alive if I cannot recover to lead an independent life. I don't want a respirator used. I don't want medicine used. I don't want to be fed. All I want are painkillers to keep me comfortable if I'm conscious. That's all.

Doctor, you know that if I were talking to you in person you couldn't treat me against my will. Well, I don't believe you can treat me against my Living Will, either. And if you do, I want my daughter to call the police and demand that you be charged with assault for treating me against my will. I also want her to sue you for every penny you've got. I certainly hope that makes my wishes clear. Are they clear to you, Inga?

Inga Hanson. Yes, Mother. I understand what you want, and while I don't necessarily agree with you, I promise that I will do my best to see that your rights are protected.

You may not be comfortable with the style of this mock script, and that's fine. I only offer it to give you an idea of the kinds of things you should say in your videotaped Living Will and the physical manner in which you should present yourself.

When you have completed your videotaped Living Will, you should have several copies of it made. (Many photo-development stores offer a videotape copying service at a reasonable price.) Give a copy of the tape to a family member and a copy to your attorney, and place one in a safe place yourself. Review the tape once a year to make sure it has not degraded. The first time you observe even a slight change in the tape, take your original and have new copies made. In addition, if you still agree with *everything* you say on the tape, drop a signed, dated note to your attorney and the family member who has a copy of the tape stating that you have reviewed it on the particular date and still agree with everything you said on the tape.

If, at any time, you find you have changed your mind about anything on the tape, ask for the return of all the copies and destroy them. The same thing goes for your written Living Will. This document and the videotaped Living Will are meant to protect your right to control your destiny. If the Living Will no longer speaks clearly for you, prepare a new one. A Living Will that contains provisions with which you do not agree is not only useless, it is dangerous.

Appendix

RESOURCES

*B*ecause the author of this book is not an attorney, there is really no getting around the fact that if you need legal advice you need to see an attorney. Do not use this book as a substitute for seeing an attorney if you need legal advice. Just as you would have an attorney review your conventional will, it makes sense to have an attorney review your Living Will. If you or your attorney need information about the legal status of Living Wills in your particular state, you can obtain specific information from two places: You can contact the office of your state attorney general, or you can write to or telephone: Concern for Dying / Society for the Right to Die, 250 West Fifty-seventh Street, New York, New York 10107, (212) 246-6973

Concern for Dying can supply you with Living Will forms and is dedicated to preserving the autonomy and rights of the dying patient. The group has a number of unique publications and services, and you might try writing for lists of publications.

And you might consider taking advantage of the group's Living Will registry. For a one-time $25 fee the group will review your Living Will and keep a registered copy on file in its New York office. The group will also send you a plastic "mini will" for your wallet, stamped with your Living Will registration number.

INDEX

141